RED EARTH, BLUE SKY

ALSO BY MARGARET RAU
MUSK OXEN

RED EARTH, BLUE SKY

THE AUSTRALIAN OUTBACK

MARGARET RAU

PHOTOGRAPHS BY THE AUTHOR

Thomas Y. Crowell
New York

FOR MY LITTLE AUSTRALIAN FRIEND AMY

I would like to express my gratitude to all those Australians both in and out of government who helped me with information, criticism, and advice. I would also like to thank Qantas personnel, who proved most helpful to me in my research.

Red Earth, Blue Sky: The Australian Outback
Copyright © 1981 by Margaret Rau

For information address
Thomas Y. Crowell Junior Books,
10 East 53rd Street,
New York, N.Y. 10022.
Published simultaneously in Canada
by Fitzhenry & Whiteside Limited, Toronto.

Library of Congress Cataloging in Publication Data

Rau, Margaret.
Red Earth, blue sky.

SUMMARY: Examines life in Australia's harsh yet
beautiful desert known as the Outback.
1. Australia—Description and travel
—Juvenile literature. 2. Australia—Social life and
customs—Juvenile literature. [1. Australia—Description
and travel. 2. Australia—Social life and customs]
I. Title
DU105.R38 1981   994   80-2457
ISBN 0-690-04080-6
ISBN 0-690-04081-4 (lib. bdg.)

1 2 3 4 5 6 7 8 9 10

First Edition

FOREWORD

In 1976 I was down under in Australia writing a book on the kangaroo. The book completed I embarked on a journey around the great continent to see as much as I could of it. I went by bus and train because only at ground level can the topography of an area be fully appreciated.

And so I came to Alice Springs in the Red Center of the Outback. I visited Ayers Rock but did not have much time to explore the surrounding country. However, going south to Adelaide over an unbelievably corrugated road in the dead of night, I was intrigued by the dark, flat wastes that spread away on all sides, lighted only by huge stars. Scarcely a light planted by man shone out in all that great platter of land.

Like many travelers before me I felt the mystery of endless space and time. I made up my mind to return one day and give more of my attention to this silent platter of seeming infinity.

So it was that in 1978 I came back to travel at leisure through that part of the Outback which stretches from Alice Springs in the center of Australia to the green coastal fringe in the south. My way took me through two states—the Northern Territory and South Australia. I was fortunate to have arrived in September, the down-under spring, after rare drenching winter rains had brought up foliage that even old-timers had never seen before.

Under the mulga trees the wilderness was spangled with a riot of tiny desert flowers. They did not last, however, as week by week the sun grew hotter and spring slid into the down-under summer. Then I experienced relentless days of brassy heat, furious gales, thunderstorms when great forked bolts of lightning danced over the plains.

I met and talked to many Outback people, both Aborigine and white. They welcomed me into their homesteads, into the little settlement of Indulkina. They entertained me in their dugout homes in Coober Pedy. Warm, hospitable, proud, they lived in isolated islands in that great sea of land.

I have not space to name all the children with whom I became friends—laughing, independent, tough, yet surprisingly gentle. They showed me their treasures: hollow eggs of desert birds, tiny sand toads, mountain dragon lizards with their scoop of freshly laid eggs beside them. They drove me to their secret spots, following rough tracks in jeeps they were almost too small to handle. Yet handle them they did. They confided to me their dreams and their fears—dreams and fears that began and ended in the great whirl of Outback.

And so I came away to write their story. If I have not done them or their land justice, it is because the subject is too immense to enclose within the covers of a single book.

CONTENTS

CORAL SEA

PACIFIC
OCEAN

GREAT BARRIER REEF

AUTHOR'S JOURNEY
THROUGH THE OUTBACK

EMILY GAP

BRISBANE

ALICE SPRINGS
ORANGE CREEK

AYERS ROCK
✕

KULGERA

TIEYON

WALES
EWCASTLE
SYDNEY

ERNABELLA

MIMILLEE

OODNADATTA

INDULKINA

GRANITE DOWNS

SOUTH AUSTRALIA

NEW RAILWAY

MANGURI
MABEL CREEK

ANNA CREEK

LAKE EYRE

COOBER PEDY

BILLA KALINA

COMMONWEALTH HILL

TASMAN SEA

NULLARBOR
PLAIN

ARCOONA

TRANSCONTINENTAL
RAILWAY

TARCOOLA

WOOMERA

PORT
AUGUSTA

CARRIETON

ORROROO

GREAT
AUSTRALIAN
BIGHT

ADELAIDE

THE ANCIENT LAND

A typical Outback scene.

The flat scarlet plains stretch away to the horizon, broken here and there by a solitary gnarled tree. With its scant covering of gray green herbiage the red earth lies burnished and gleaming beneath the blistering sun. Overhead hangs the great inverted bowl of blue sky. There is no cloud in it, no breath of air in the hot still land. Time seems to have died.

This is typical Australian Outback, bush country. It covers one million square miles of space which includes most of the states of Western Australia, the Northern Territory and South Australia as well as parts of New South Wales and Queensland. This semiarid land is interspersed with great stretches of desert—the Simpson Desert, the Stony Desert, the Gibson Desert, the Victoria Desert—where scarcely anything can find root.

In the vast expanse rise a few scattered ranges of craggy hills.

Chains of sand dunes—some red, others pale ivory—stretch for miles across the plain. The sand hills are either bare or clothed with tall native cypress pine, with stunted, gnarled mulga and graceful myall trees, both Australian forms of acacia. Long expanses of plain are strewn with small rock chips. They are known as the gibber plains. Blue-green saltbush, blue bush, and tall old man blue bush dot the plain.

In a million square miles of space there are bound to be different kinds of flora. Cane grass grows thick in swampy places. Limestone country gives birth to spiky spinifex. Now and then open stands of mulga trees appear, uninterrupted except by an occasional bent desert oak, one of the oldest of living plants. In the hill ranges, where a little more rain falls, trees and brush grow more thickly.

Here and there the Outback is punctuated by low, flat-topped mesas and rocky ridges that break the monotony of the skyline.

Few if any permanent creeks or rivers cross the surface of the Outback. Those that do are at best just strings of water holes. During long dry spells these disappear altogether. Yet there is water. It flows unseen in underground streams, their courses marked by a tracery of trees—eucalyptus, among them the species known as the coolabah, and shrubs of various sizes including the tea tree—which sink their roots down to the moisture below.

Little change can be expected in a country that averages only four to six inches of rainfall a year. Rarely heavy rains drench the

Above: In the parching heat of the day, cattle seek the shelter of trees. Set in a row, the trees mark the course of an underground stream.
Below: Trees beside a water hole bring an oasis of beauty to an ordinarily treeless plain.

land in the winter months, which in this down-under continent are June, July, and August. Then, when September brings in the brief spring, the red plains become colorful meadowlands for a few weeks. Thousands upon thousands of flowers—tiny white and yellow daisies, brittle white pompoms of everlastings, purple parakilya, and scarlet Sturt peas—create a vast, delicate mosaic.

This is one of the best times of the year and the creatures of the Outback take advantage of it. All the members of the strange Australian lizard family come out to bask in the sunlight. Flocks of pink-and-gray galahs burst chattering through the sky. The galah, Australia's most common parrot, is unique to this continent, which boasts some sixty species, many of which make their homes in the Outback.

Kangaroos bound over the grassy meadows or sprawl in the shade of the trees or mulga scrub. More rarely the great wingless emus, cousins to the ostrich, strut across the flat plains with awkward dignity. They walk in groups of twos and threes, their heads stretched at the end of long necks, their tail plumes wagging like feather dusters.

Left: An Australian lizard called a goanna rises out of his hole to bask in the sunlight.
Right: Red kangaroos, well-known inhabitants of the Outback.

In two or three weeks the heat slams down again and the magical spring world is burned away. Animals and humans must again make do within a barren land.

Above the flat platter of plain, knotty outcroppings of sandstone stand like sentinels. The most remarkable of these is the wind-and-rain-polished monolith known as Ayers Rock, long considered sacred by the Aborigines of the vicinity. The outcroppings are the work of millennia of winds and rains. They have washed away the less durable soil to expose the ribs of this oldest and flattest land mass in the world—the island-continent of Australia.

Most of Australia's population of some fourteen million people live along the country's green coastal fringe. Here stand her largest cities—Sydney, Melbourne, Newcastle, Brisbane, Darwin, Perth, and Adelaide. The people who live in the coastal cities have seldom if ever visited the Outback and usually know little about it. It is a world apart from their safe, ordered lives—harsh, beautiful, secretive, a land of immense distances and silences.

The Outback was not always so. Millennia ago the lowest portions formed the floor of a sea that stretched far inland. Forests and jungle growth made the surrounding land green. There were many freshwater lakes. The ancestors of Australia's varied marsupial family throve here. There were giant possums, huge marsupial lions, and kangaroos. Great wombatlike creatures as big as cows called diprotodons lived there too.

Nothing definite is known about the early history of man upon the continent. Anthropologists have reconstructed the arrival of the first Aborigines, which they believe was some thirty thousand years ago during the last world ice age. They came by boat following a series of low-lying islands that stretched between Asia and Australia like stepping-stones. By the time they arrived, the sea had probably receded from the Outback. The forests and jungles had given way to sweeping savannas. The lakes in the Outback were beginning to shrink. But there was still plenty of game.

For some twenty thousand years the migrations continued. Some of the Aborigines brought dogs, which became the ancestors of the present-day dingoes. Then, as the ice age drew to a close and ice caps around the world began to melt, the sea rose, inundating many of the stepping-stone islands and nibbling away at the shores of Australia. The continent became completely isolated, and its unique plant and animal life developed.

The Aborigines continued their nomadic existence hunting and gathering their food. Those who had remained in the coastal areas had a relatively easy time of it. But those who had wandered into the Outback found life becoming more and more difficult as the country began entering its present dry cycle. The freshwater lakes evaporated altogether or turned salt. Streams disappeared as rainfall dwindled. Food became scarce.

The Outback Aborigines met the challenge by living as simply as possible. They wore no clothing and carried only a few necessary possessions. The men had barbed wooden hunting spears and hollowed-out spear throwers, which could also serve as dishes. Fitted with a flake of fine-grained stone at one end, the thrower could be used as a cutting tool too. Some tribes carried boomerangs. A boomerang is a hunting stick that may be about thirty inches long. It can be thrown with deadly accuracy. One kind is made from thin hardwood and is curved so that if it misses its mark it will return to the owner. The women of the tribes carried wooden dishes, string bags which they wove from plant fibers, digging sticks, and two grinding stones to pound grass seeds into flour.

Whenever they could, the Aborigines pitched their camps near water holes. Their houses, called wurleys or humpies, were made of desert tree branches crisscrossed to form flimsy frameworks, which were covered with bark and leaves and dirt. The wurleys were built with their backs to the wind and their entrances facing east. The hunters slept at the doorways so that the first daylight would waken them and send them off for game.

While the men hunted, the women searched the plains for other kinds of food. They gathered the edible seeds of various desert plants and grasses, wild yams and onions and the roots of certain young trees. They picked the tiny wild desert fruits and berries and nuts that ripened in season. They collected the galls on the mulga

The remains of an old wurley or humpie, an early Aboriginal shelter. Today most of the wurlies have been replaced by corrugated iron or tin sheds.

and the bloodwood trees. They followed the faint tracks of the smaller Outback creatures and snared them in their holes—snakes, the large goanna, a monitor lizard whose flesh is as sweet as that of a chicken, and the Australian marsupial, the bandicoot.

They knew where to dig under the coolabah trees for witchetty grubs—big, fat, sluglike creatures that when roasted and shucked of tail, head, and skin taste as sweet and bland as butter. And they knew how to locate the hills of the honey ants whose bellies are swollen with sweet honey, and how to follow a wilderness bee to its hive tucked away in some tree.

If they became thirsty they knew which trees could be tapped to provide water and where to dig in a dry creek bed to bring up a seepage of moisture. What they hunted or gathered they brought back to their communal camp and shared with one another. There was always food. But if the hunters managed to bag a large kangaroo, there would be a great feasting with perhaps singing and dancing as well—a corroboree.

Poor as the Aborigines' material possessions might be, they lived a life rich in myth. They felt themselves a part of the vast, harsh desert in the way that the animals and plants are part of it—not to exploit it but to live in harmony with it.

Each tribe or individual claimed kinship with some plant or animal which in dream or trance was supposed to act as guard or guide. Each tribe had its own myths that centered around its cult heroes whose deeds were performed in a long-ago time—the Dreamtime. But to the Aborigine the Dreamtime does not lie in the past alone. It is ever present beneath the trappings of the outer world. The men believed that by dancing and chanting the sacred words they could enter the Dreamtime and accompany the ancient heroes on their external exploits. But to do this they had to be initiated into the secrets of the tribe. At the age of fourteen, male children went through severe initiation rites. These prepared them to participate in the secret ceremonies that were open only to men.

Women also had their secret dances. Some of these dances were performed to draw spirit children into their wombs. The women believed that they became pregnant only when such a spirit entered their bodies.

The Aborigines attributed illnesses to magical causes. In central Australia their most powerful magic consisted of singing a curse while pointing with a dead man's bone in the direction of the victim. Only the tribal medicine men were believed to have the power to deflect the curse with their own rituals.

The tribe was governed by elders who laid down the laws according to the visions they saw during trance times. Those who broke the taboos or offended the elders could expect a visit from the dread kurdaitcha man, the tribal executioner. He was supposed to have great cunning. He wore shoes made of marsupial fur, bound with string and lined with emu feathers. On these soft feathers he could slither over the land leaving no tracks behind him as he searched out his prey. Few escaped his deadly spear.

The most terrifying kurdaitcha of all was not a human being but Kurdimurkra, the terrible demon whose home was the desert sand hills. He rode the dusty willy-willies—miniature whirlwinds created by heat that dance over the land like dervishes. He was also said to mount the fierce sandstorms that blot out the sun and fill the day with midnight darkness. When he was out hunting, someone would surely die.

Death was always feared by the Aborigines. They believed that when a person died his soul might linger around the living and cause harm. So the burial rites were carefully observed. Afterward everything used by the dead person was destroyed to break all linkage with the living. The wurley where the death occurred was torn apart, and the whole camp would break up and move on to a new spot.

An old shack, once the home of Aborigines and now deserted because a murder took place inside its walls.

At the time the British arrived on the shores of Australia and began colonization, there were more than five hundred tribes of Aborigines with as many different languages. Each followed its own customs and rites. But the tribes were small. On the whole continent, which is about the size of the United States, there were only some three hundred thousand Aborigines.

2

THE SETTLERS

A young boy stands in front of an early settler's kitchen and saddle shed.

In 1770 Captain James Cook landed at Botany Bay, New South Wales, and took formal possession of eastern Australia on August 23 for the British government. Sixteen years later the government appointed the eastern coast of Australia as a place to which convicts might be transported. The First Fleet, under the command of Captain Arthur Phillip and consisting of about 720 convicts and 110 marines and officers, arrived in Botany Bay in January 1788.

From then on there was a steady flow of immigrants. In the beginning they were convicts. Later they were ordinary settlers. It was a strange, lonely life for the newcomers, who had many adjustments to make. One was to the Australian seasons. Because the continent lies in the southern hemisphere its seasons are exactly opposite to those above the equator. So the colonists discovered that their coldest period now fell in July and August, while Christmas came in the middle of summer heat.

Animals and plants were all different too. The colonists found kangaroos in place of their familiar deer, eucalyptuses instead of oaks and maple trees and poplars. They were afraid of the Aboriginal peoples around them whose ways they did not understand.

As they began occupying the fertile lands along the coast they encroached on the ancestral lands of these strange dark people. The Aborigines tried to fight back. But their weapons were crude and could not match the guns of the invaders. Many were massacred. The rest fled. Colonization went forward steadily.

Inland occupation, however, was much slower because explorations revealed a vast barren land, harsh and cruel, so lacking in rainfall that farming was useless. This was what came to be known as the Outback. Only after sheep were introduced to Australia did the Outback seem to carry possibilities. Then there was a scramble to obtain land.

Outback lands are public lands held by the government, which leases out parcels to applicants. In the early 1920s a number of one-hundred-square-mile lots were leased out along with cash grants to help with development. Men who were almost penniless took out leases, put up hovels for living quarters, and invested in a few sheep. With such small, barren holdings they could not hope to survive. During the early 1930s, when cattle began coming in, men with money in their pockets bought out the small leaseholders. The hundred-square-mile lots were joined together bit by bit to form large-size holdings of three to four thousand square miles.

It was a rough, brutal life. Many of the early stations, as the holdings were called, were stocked with cattle obtained by rustling, or paddy dodging as it is known in central Australia. Aborigines made up some of the work force. Deprived of their hunting grounds, they had begun camping around the new settlements, exchanging labor for a little cash and food supplies for themselves and their families.

With their keen powers of observation the Aborigines could easily track straying cattle. They also became able horsemen, skilled at mustering, roping, and branding. They had one drawback. Now and then, stirred by the spirit of the vast, empty plains, they would suddenly decide to go on long, lonely treks—walkabouts—that might take them away for two or three months at a time.

The early homesteads of the settlers in the Outback were adobe huts made of spinifex mixed with mud or, when they could get the material, corrugated iron sheds. To such cramped quarters rough adventurers sometimes brought young brides. The women had to be of as stern material as the men. Often they stayed alone for months at a time while the men went out on cattle musters, as roundups are called in Australia. Chance visitors were few. Once a month a horse or camel train might show up with mail and supplies hauled from Adelaide.

Too frequently the women had to bear their children without outside help. On top of their many other chores, they had to care for the ill with only a few home remedies at hand. If there was a serious accident—a broken back or ruptured spleen—the victim had to be hauled by horse over rutted trails to some small bush clinic hundreds of miles away. Often the person died before reaching it. Common childhood maladies also resulted in numerous deaths. Here and there in the melancholy plains, a white tombstone marks some small grave that broke a woman's heart.

In 1911 a Presbyterian minister by the name of John Flynn traveled through the Outback on church business. He was shocked by the lack of medical aid for the people who lived there and made up his mind to do something about it. With the end of World War I, as the airplane became increasingly important, the Reverend Mr. Flynn realized how useful it would be either to airlift patients to hospitals or to bring in doctors to treat them. He began to talk about his dream to others.

One of the men he talked to was Hudson Fysh, founder of Qantas. This is Australia's national airline. The name Qantas comes from the initials of "Queensland and Northern Territory Aerial Service." In 1927 Qantas provided Flynn with his first air ambulance, a de Havilland DH50A.

But the air ambulance was only half the story. Rapid communication between Outback and air base was needed. This was provided by a young Australian radio engineer named Alfred Traeger. He invented a transmitting–receiving set driven by bicycle pedals, which could put doctor and patient in instant communication with each other.

As time went by the transceiver sets were improved. More and more were manufactured and placed in isolated stations. Today a modern radio network covers the Outback, taking the place of telephones. Using the transceiver sets doctors and patients can be in immediate touch with each other. Nurses ride the ambulance planes with the doctors and run little clinics in tiny Outback towns. Nurses and doctors working together staff what is known as the Royal Flying Doctor Service.

To ease the isolation the women felt so keenly, the Flying Doctor Service started setting aside definite hours each day during which the women could use the transceiver sets to chat with one another, exchanging comfort, advice, and family news, breaking the monotony of their lives. This service still continues. The network also receives and transmits business telegrams for the Outback people.

Correspondence school has always been available to isolated Australian children. Textbooks and assignments are provided by the Board of Education headquarters in the various States. In the old days pupils in the Outback got their assignments by the slow camel mail train. Parents helped with the lessons. Completed exercises went back by camel to be graded. It might be months before the pupils got the results or heard from their teachers. In the meantime interest flagged and school work suffered. Even if lessons were completed adequately, children grew up with no contact at all with the outside world.

A woman named Adelaide Meitke changed this by urging that

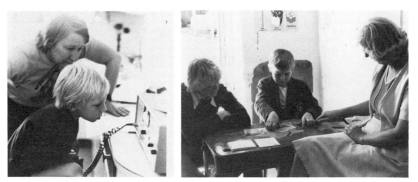

Left: Class is in session for this six-year-old child of the Outback. With his mother, he waits his turn to recite over the School of the Air two-way radio.
Right: A young student and his governess (left) are visited by his School of the Air teacher.

the Flying Doctor network be used for a School of the Air, which would bring teachers in personal contact with their students. The first School of the Air program was broadcast in 1951. Today there are twelve School of the Air bases in Australia, servicing all the children in the Outback. Most of the time the children's only contact with their teacher is over the air. But periodically teachers travel to Outback stations to visit with the children individually and to get to know them better.

With the passage of years other means have also helped to break the complete isolation of the past. Modern automobiles and even a few small private planes diminish distances. But isolation still plays a big part in Outback life. The highway that connects Adelaide in the south to Alice Springs in the center is in places only a rutted dirt road, punishing to engines and tires. And the narrow dirt roads that snake away from it often meander fifty miles or more before reaching the station. Blowouts and engine trouble, roads that in wet weather turn into bogs miring cars—all are serious threats.

The crude sheds of the early pioneers have given way to rambling buildings of stone or brick. They stand among lawns and vegetable and flower gardens shaded with tall trees, looking like green oases in the tawny desert lands. The homestead itself is skirted with wide verandas. Doors and windows are arranged to create through drafts to help the occupants survive the furnace-hot summers.

Besides the homestead, which is the headquarters of the vast grazing lands that surround it, there are barracks for station hands. A small chiller contains stores of meat and a good supply of groceries because the nearest market may be well over fifty miles away. There is a garage where the station mechanics can repair the trucks, jeeps, family cars, and motorcycles. All the buildings are made of stone, brick or corrugated iron due to the scarcity of wood in the Outback.

Galvanized iron water tanks stand on stilts near the homestead. A windmill run by wind or, on still days, by a small motor, draws the water out of a bore and into a ground tank. From there it is pumped into the overhead tanks. The pressure is enough to draw the water down into pipes that service kitchen, bathroom, and laundry room.

Often this main supply of water is too brackish to use for anything other than bathing and washing dishes and clothes. Ground-level tanks placed under the eaves of the house catch the runoff from the sparse rains. These tanks provide fresh water for cooking and drinking.

Old-fashioned wood stoves are still very much in use in the homestead kitchens. But there are usually also modern stoves fueled by cylinders of gas. The wood stoves may provide the hot water for the homestead. A water tank stands just outside the kitchen wall opposite the stove. The water from the tank circulates through a series of pipes looped against the back of the stove. As the water is recycled the whole tankful becomes boiling hot.

At some stations hot water is obtained by manually filling a forty-four-gallon drum set over an incinerator. A fire in the incinerator heats the water, which is then piped into the house. This means the supply of hot water is always limited.

Finding wood for fuel is a real problem in this almost barren land, especially now that the government protects the few stands of trees that remain. Some stations are beginning to solve the problem by using solar heating. They have installed water pipes in their roofs on which the tropical sun beats down almost without letup the year round. The pipes provide enough hot water for nine to eleven consecutive months.

Electricity is provided by station generators. Many of the stations still use the weak 32-volt-power engines. These cannot produce sufficient power for such things as air conditioners, toasters, and floor heaters. Refrigerators and freezers are run with gas. The more powerful 240-volt engines can provide most modern conveniences, but also consume greater amounts of fuel. To save energy and expense the generator is turned off at night or switched to low voltage.

The schoolroom is one of the most important places in any station. Sometimes it is in the homestead itself. If at all possible it is located in a separate room. It is usually run by a governess who is paid from a small allowance the government provides for this purpose.

The governesses are almost always young women who have just graduated from high school or perhaps college and are trying to decide what to do with their lives. Their salaries are small, but they have free board and room with the household and are treated as family members. Some cannot endure the loneliness and do not stay long. Others thrive on it.

Marie Walsh is one of these governesses. She is a tall, slender fair-haired girl nineteen years old. She comes from green Kangaroo Island off the southern coast of Australia. And this is her second year as governess on Tieyon Station. She plans to put in one more year to qualify for child-care courses at the Alice Springs hospital.

Marie teaches eleven-year-old Vicki Smith and her eight-year-old brother, Jamie, whose father owns Tieyon Station. The children's schoolroom is sunny and airy with two desks, one for each child, a desk for Marie and a table where the youngest Smith child, four-year-old Jay, can do some coloring when he wanders in.

The children start school at nine o'clock. They spend the first hour in a review session of multiplication tables, spelling, and reading. At ten o'clock they break for recess and flock into the homestead kitchen for smoko time. Smoko time is the Australian equivalent of the coffee break.

At half past ten the children return to their schoolroom. It's time for Jamie's session with his teacher at School of the Air. Tieyon Station is in the Northern Territory so his School of the Air base is in Alice Springs. Jamie takes his place in front of the radio transceiver set. It will put him in direct contact with the main transmitting and receiving equipment at the Alice Springs headquarters.

Jamie's transceiver crackles to life as he holds the microphone in one hand. The teacher is going through the roll call of her third-grade students. When she comes to Jamie's name he pushes the transmitting button and says, "Good morning, Jamie here. Over."

"Over" means he is finished speaking. He immediately pushes the button in his microphone, leaving the line open for his teacher's reply. During Jamie's session, which lasts for twenty minutes, each child has a turn at reciting or giving some news or answering a few questions about the subject matter.

Finally Jamie says "over" for the last time and returns to his desk and his schoolwork. It will be Vicki's turn in the afternoon.

The Smith children like Friday best. Then Marie often takes them on nature walks to the dry creek bed which lies nearby. Sometimes, instead, they go by motorbike to the chain of low hills that scallop the horizon a half mile away. Leaving their motorbikes at the foot of the hills, they climb the slopes to explore the caves dug by early Aborigines for shelter.

All about them lies the great, flat platter of land, swimming out to the horizon as far as the eye can see. The little cluster of homestead buildings looks like tossed blocks in the immensity.

There is empty distance everywhere. It is a familiar sight to all Out-back children. Many of them feel closed in and homesick in moun-tainous places where steep slopes and tall trees obstruct their view on all sides.

With their governess Marie Walsh, the three Smith children and a little girl visitor go for a nature walk along a creek bed. The creek bed, not only dry but undistinguishable during the dry season, will flood during rains.

3

LIFE ON A CATTLE STATION

A small boy delights in helping his parents muster a small herd of cattle.

A day on a cattle station in the Outback starts anywhere from four to seven in the morning. Breakfast usually consists of steak, eggs, toast, and coffee prepared by the manager's or the owner's wife. She usually cooks all the meals for the household and sometimes for the station hands as well.

Meals are hearty. It is a matter of steak, or some kind of beef, served three times a day with potatoes, tinned or fresh vegetables, salad if it is available, bread, dessert, and coffee. There is always plenty of powdered milk, which is used instead of fresh milk because dairy cows mean extra work in a crowded day.

Occasionally the woman will go with her husband to repair bores or help with the cattle. But usually while he is out taking care of station work, she will be keeping the homestead running, doing housework, perhaps teaching the children, answering telegrams and letters. She will see that the outgoing mail is driven to the nearest highway stop. There it is placed in the empty gasoline drum, which serves as the station's mail box, to be taken by the bus driver on his way to Alice Springs. Once a week, usually on Friday, he will also deliver mail, which again has to be picked up.

If there is a governess she may volunteer her help with meals, dishes, and housecleaning. A mechanic and his apprentice are usually employed to repair cars, trucks, and motorcycles, to build yards, and to fix windmills. Often there is a yardman to keep the place neat and the grass green, and to tend the vegetable and flower gardens. Like as not he is an old man on pension who cannot get the Outback out of his system.

The station hands are made up of seasoned stockmen, younger less-experienced station hands, and apprentices. These are usually young people in their teens. The male apprentices are called jackeroos, the female ones are called jilleroos. After four years of apprenticeship they become full-fledged station hands. The Aboriginal apprentices are called ringers. There are usually eight or more station hands. Most of them are single, though a few may bring their wives.

Aboriginal ringers, adept horsemen, on a cattle station. Note the water tank and windmill in the background, a common sight on Outback stations.

Twice a year, winter and summer, there is a general cattle muster. The big muster takes place in winter because then the

cattle are easier to handle and it is pleasanter for the musterers. Mustering is done primarily to gather the cattle together to select those in prime condition—fats as they are called in Australia. They will be freighted to abattoirs in Alice Springs or Adelaide. The mustering also nets new calves, which are branded. Male calves are castrated. This turns them into steers, which develop into better beef.

Mustering may be done with horses, motorcycles, jeeps, light trucks, and even helicopters and planes. David Smith of Tieyon Station uses a Cessna 172. From overhead he can spot the cattle and flush them out of hidden thickets. He claims that this cuts mustering time by two or three months.

However, horses are the backbone of mustering. Young recruits usually break in their own animals. Once a horse is broken in, it is used by the person who trained it. Each musterer has two teams of six horses each. One team is worked for six weeks. Then it is turned loose in the horse paddocks to rest and the other team is used. Four of the six horses are used to walk the cattle. The other two horses are for specialized work. One is the camp horse, used to cut out selected cattle. The other is the night horse, trained to round up cattle after dark in case of a stampede, or rush, as it is called in Australia.

Station horses being mustered for selection of work teams. In the corrals each station hand will cut out his own team for use in cattle mustering.

A head stockman is in charge of the camp. Since the men may be out mustering for five or six months at a time, they are accompanied by a truck or caravan which carries the food supplies, called tucker by Outback Australians. In the old days tucker used to consist of salt meat and dry bread.

Today the trucks are equipped with refrigerators so that a variety of food can be provided, though the main course is almost always steak. Sometimes the camp takes along its own cook. More often the musterers take turns preparing the meals.

The truck also carries the men's swags. A swag is made up of a camp sheet, which is a large square of canvas, a mattress, and some blankets. These are all rolled up together and held in place with a leather strap and a buckle. At night the buckle is undone and the swag is unrolled to provide a bed. The canvas sheet acts as a layer between the mattress and the ground. In case of cold or rainy weather it can also be wrapped around the sleeper to keep off rain.

Scattered throughout the station are bores topped by windmills that draw up water and spill it into drinking troughs for the cattle. Water holes in dry creek beds and dams built across depressions to hold rain are other sources of water. If heavy rains fill these catchment areas they may contain water for as long as two years.

Cattle never stray too far from the watering places and most of them tend to stick together in groups. It is the job of the musterers to round up the groups and unite them into one big herd, or mob as it is called in the Outback.

The mob will include steers, bullocks, bulls, cows, calves, and heifers. Some will be fat, others skinny. Occasionally the musterers will flush a wild bull out of the brush. There are many such wild cattle who have managed to escape the musterers year after year. They are shy and rambunctious, and when they take to their heels they can carry along half the cattle with them. If they are coerced into the herd they may cause havoc. Then it is necessary to shoot them.

Once a mob is collected it is merely a matter of walking it from watering place to watering place until it reaches the station yards. Usually the watering places are eight to ten miles apart. That is a day's journey for the cattle, which graze leisurely as they go.

Above: Musterers start out for a day's work. They will roam the plains to round up straying cattle and bring them in for trucking to the Alice Springs abbatoirs.
Below: These cattle are on the last leg of their journey to the pens to be shipped out.

The key watering places each have an enclosed yard into which the cattle can be driven. Otherwise a watch would have to be kept over them at night to prevent them from straying. In the yards prime cattle can be cut out from the rest and the calves branded and castrated.

Once the cattle reach the station yards there is one last chore before they can be trucked off. They must be tail tagged with the identification mark of the station. After they have gone through the abattoirs their carcasses are checked for tuberculosis and brucellosis. If any show a positive reaction the government disposes of the carcasses and notifies the owner, who will be recompensed. The Department of Agriculture then investigates to see if the owner's station has been carrying out its own program of periodic testing and eradication of infected cattle. This is required by law.

Left: Cows brought in for fattening are being spayed by the local veterinarian, assisted by a young woman station hand.
Right: A small boy helps keep the cattle moving as they are herded onto the truck that will carry them off to market.

During mustering time the manager or owner commutes between station and stock camp. Sometimes he helps with the mustering. He also spends a lot of time checking the fences and the bores to be sure the windmills are working. He makes minor repairs if necessary and goes for help if major work is required. During the busiest seasons it may be midnight before he sits down to his evening meal.

All the major decisions are his. He has to figure out costs before ordering such improvements as new bores and the laying of new pipelines to dry areas. He has to decide whether it will be profitable to buy skinny cattle from other stations in order to fatten them on his own land and then sell them. If there are sub-standard cows among the purchased cattle he will have to call in a veterinarian to help him with the spaying, so that the cows will not produce Grade B calves.

Largest of all the cattle stations in Australia is the Anna Creek

Cattle Station. It covers some eleven thousand square miles and is the largest cattle area under one management in the world. For twenty-six years Richard Nunn has been in charge of the property, which is owned by the Kidman Enterprises. Richard and his wife, Connie, have brought up their nine children here. Four are married and gone now. But five are still living at home.

Seventeen-year-old Anna is the station cook. She has completed secondary school in Adelaide, but it was a wrench for her to leave home. This is true of most Outback children when they are suddenly transported from the wide open spaces of the stations to the bustling crowded city, where people are not so friendly. Anna was dreadfully homesick, especially so in the strict disciplines of the boarding school, so different from the free and easy atmosphere of the homestead. She could hardly wait for holidays so that she could return to it. And she cried bitterly every time she had to go back.

Though she is presently station cook Anna looks on this as merely an interim job while she sorts out her future. Eventually she hopes to find something that will take her into the outside world— perhaps as a stewardess with a shipping company. She wants to exchange the vast red platter of inland sea for the blue expanses of the ocean with which she became acquainted while she was in Adelaide.

Meanwhile Anna is tackling the problem of feeding large numbers of people—never less than fifteen and sometimes as many as thirty. Planning is the hardest part because Anna can't run to the corner grocery when she gives out of supplies. There is always meat. If the chiller is empty someone will slaughter a bullock and cut it up. But vegetables are difficult to get. They come from the garden which a pensioner, old Bert, tends. And once they are gone there is nowhere to turn for fresh supplies.

There are some fifty chickens on the place, but they are either too old to produce many eggs or the goannas that swarm through the country in the summertime steal them. That does not matter to Anna's father. He does not keep the chickens to provide food. They are his pets along with the geese, the ducks, the silky bantams, the guinea fowl, and the turkey. He won't let anyone kill them, though he will permit a goose and a couple of ducks to be sacrificed for Christmas dinner.

The Nunn children have always been amused by their father's affection for birds of all kinds. He keeps canaries, budgies, a seventeen-year-old white cockatoo, some homing pigeons, and five peacocks. He depends on the peacocks, geese, and guinea fowl to rouse him with their squacking whenever anyone comes prowling around the place at night. They are better than his watch dogs, he says.

Nineteen-year-old Eddie Nunn does the odd jobs around the station and helps the mechanic with repair work. Like his father he is interested in horses. Richard Nunn is proud of the thoroughbred that he has raised. It is a great race horse and Eddie is always the jockey. Between them they have won trophy after trophy at the race meets all over this part of Australia.

Eighteen-year-old Richard Nunn is head stockman at one of the camps. The young people under him are all teenagers like himself. Rich makes a good stockman. He runs a tight camp and at the same time manages to keep the affection of his crew. His father depends on his trustworthiness.

Fifteen-year-old Jan is a jilleroo in her brother's camp. She loves Anna Creek Station so much that nothing can get her to leave home and attend school in Adelaide. She started correspondence courses at home but when she turned fifteen and was no longer required by Australian law to go to school, she quit her studies in favor of station work.

Like Jan, fourteen-year-old Margaret does not want to leave the station and is also taking correspondence courses at home. She loves horses and during weekends and vactions she likes to go out as a temporary jilleroo just to get in her quota of riding. But next year Margaret will tear herself away from the station and

Fifteen-year-old Jan Nunn (far right) with Aborigines on a tractor at her family's cattle station, Anna Creek, where she is a jilleroo.

go to Adelaide to attend a school that gives rural courses. She wants to become a veterinarian. But it won't be an easy position to find, no matter how good her qualifications. Veterinarian jobs are few and highly coveted.

Connie Nunn worries about her children's future, especially Jan's because she has dropped her education altogether.

"It's not as though you children will inherit this place," she tells the girl. "Your father is only the manager. One day he will retire. What will happen to you then?"

Sometimes Connie looks back with regret at the years of devotion the whole family has given to this harsh lonely land. All they have to show for it now are their individual names bestowed by her husband on every outcropping and salt lake and billabong on the vast property.

Despite its size Anna Creek Station can support only some twenty thousand head of cattle. From the air the vast expanse of flat red land unreels below—the olive-green stitchery of coolabah, box, and mulga trees marking the courses of dry creek beds. Principal among them is Anna Creek, with its sister fork, after which the station is named.

Sand dunes freckled with stunted trees and scrub lie like ribs along the face of the land and are interspersed here and there with stretches of brush-strewn meadows where recent rains have fallen. These give way to a broken, barren land seamed into angry crimson corrugations by winds and flash floods—desolate wastes so pitiless they have been called Moon Country.

Occasionally a boiling hot spring bubbling up from the artesian basin of water that underlies the area has created wide marshlands. But the soil is so impregnated with sulfur that only some reeds and a few scrawny trees find root there.

Small salt lakes and ponds are scattered about like pewter mirrors. But Lake Eyre, upon which Anna Creek Station borders, is about ninety miles in length and forty-seven miles wide. It is the biggest natural inland sea in Australia.

For many years it was just a dry salt pan over which cars could race. Then in 1972 heavy rains fell to the north and east, flooding the Cooper and Diamantina rivers. They emptied their waters into the lake, filling it to overflowing. This great expanse of shallow water, which was only some twenty-one feet in depth, began responding with daily tides to the pull of the moon.

The rivers brought fish to the lake. They spawned and bred. Soon hundreds of pelicans made their homes about the shores and fished the waters.

Then the rivers dried up. Only an occasional flow from local rains fed the lake. It started to evaporate much faster than the small input of fresh water. The stagnant water became too salty for the fish to survive. Every tide cast them up by the millions until the whole margin of the lake was ringed with stinking fish. The pelicans flew away, leaving the waters completely devoid of life. Like a giant iridescent opal the lake lies now in delicate shades of purples and magentas set in the vivid red desert.

It is this desolate country that Jan loves so much. She enjoys visiting the homestead and seeing family and guests, but she is always eager to get back to the solitude of the stock camp. After every visit she and her brother are up at first daybreak—well before the rest of the family. By sunrise they are off with their crew of musterers. Their tucker does not go aboard a truck but on a wagon drawn by camels. Anna Creek is the only station that still uses camels. According to Dick Nunn camels, unlike mechanical vehicles, have the advantage of not using gas or breaking down far from the station house.

Jan and Richard find the down-under spring one of the pleasantest times for mustering, especially if there have been good rains. Then billabongs, small ponds, and dams brim with water. The beautiful blue-feathered white-faced heron arrives to build its nest, a flimsy creation of sticks stuck in the branch of a eucalyptus tree that overhangs the water.

Gaudy parrots bustle chattering everywhere. Flocks of green budgigars fly down from the north to nest in the hollows of trees. Passing through a copse down by the creek, Jan and Rich see every knothole suddenly blossom with a little green head poking out to take a look at them.

Intent on her work Jan rides quietly along. None of the musterers talk much while they are working. In silence they suffer the tormenting flies, which the warmth brings out in swarms everywhere in the Outback. The flies attack eyes and nostrils. They even fly into open mouths.

The musterers relax only when the cattle are finally in the yards. Then they can stretch out and enjoy their mealtime, which is an unhurried affair. Afterward, stomachs filled, muscles unknotted, they can laugh and talk the night away, telling tall tales, each one trying to top the other.

Generally Jan is too tired to take part in this banter. She is usually in her swag by eight o'clock. Overhead the night glitters with stars or lies caught in a web of moonlight. Far off a dingo starts howling. Now and then a rush of wind flaps over the shadowy plains like the sweep of a great bird's wings. And as the orange glow of the musterers' bonfire dies away, loneliness rises in a tide out of the great, still land.

4

THE PEOPLE OF INDULKINA

Aboriginal students giving a sing-song with their teacher. [The child in the back row, far left, is a Caucasian, son of one of the teachers. The other towheads in the group are all aborigines.] The tow-headed Aborigine child is a common sight and is apparently not always due to interracial unions.

The spread of the Europeans throughout Australia marked a rapid decline for the Aborigines. Wholesale massacres, new diseases, and the uprooting of old established ways caused their original numbers, estimated at some 300,000, to dwindle rapidly. With the loss of their homelands, tribes could no longer follow the old nomadic way of life. They began breaking up, or disappearing altogether. People were already speaking of the Aborigines as a vanishing race.

Central Australia was the last stronghold of the Aborigines, most of whom belonged to the Pitjantjatjara or Yangkuntjatjara tribes. They had been spared at first because the land was so inhospitable. But as time went by, more and more pastoralists moved in and laid claim to large tracts of Outback that the Aborigines already occupied.

The newcomers assumed that the nomadic Aborigines could

move elsewhere. After all there was still plenty of land left. Few understood that the Aborigine was a nomad only within his own territory, large as that might be. He regarded it as his ancestral home in a very special and spiritual way. He believed his ancestors had sprung from the soil of this territory and that he must die on it to be whole. When he was forced away his spiritual ties were severed. To him it was more painful than a physical amputation. He became dispirited and hopeless.

Some people began worrying about the plight of these dispossessed Aborigines, among them missionaries. They started establishing missions where they could provide medical care, food, and education, as well as religious instruction for them. One of the most successful of these missions is Ernabella, founded in 1933 for the Pitjantjatjara tribe, which lives in the vicinity of Ayers Rock.

The missionaries at Ernabella learned the Pitjantjatjara tongue so they could speak to The People, as the Pitjantjatjara refer to themselves in English. At the same time they developed a written form of the language and taught The People to read and write it. Then they translated parts of the Bible and some hymns and began holding Christian services. In 1940 they opened a school for the children. In everything they did they were careful not to disturb the tribal customs and laws that governed The People. They realized that without the anchor of their age-old traditions the Aborigines would be completely rootless.

Today the little community of some three hundred and fifty people is run by an Aboriginal council. Outsiders, whom The People call Those Others, are admitted only to teach some skill such as mechanics, building, gardening, shopkeeping, or handicrafts. The aim of the settlement is to be completely self-supporting.

Ernabella has become the model for the six or so Aboriginal settlements that have been opened by the government in the area. Indulkina, which is one of them, was founded about ten years ago. Here the Aborigines are free to settle and govern their community in their own way.

The days of low pay for Aboriginal station hands are over. New laws require equal pay for equal work. Many cattle and sheep people have responded by letting Aboriginal help go. A concerned government fills the gap by giving subsidies to those Aborigines who cannot manage for themselves. It also builds settlement houses for them. However, most of The People like simple sheds, which they make out of tin or corrugated iron. The sheds are used mainly for storage because The People have always lived in the open and most of them still prefer to do so.

The houses are used for shelter only when the weather is wet or cold. The women seldom cook on the new gas stoves in their kitchens. They feel more comfortable with an outdoor camp fire where they put on a pot of stew. While it is bubbling away the men, women, and children cluster around the fire laughing and joking, singing and spinning yarns in the old way. Anyone is welcome at the family feast, for it is Aboriginal tradition to share with one another.

Some seven years ago an elementary school was built in Indulkina. In the first three grades the children learn to read and write in their native Pitjantjatjara tongue, the only language most of their parents speak. The curriculum and textbooks the class uses have been worked out by the fifty-seven or so teachers in the reserve schools of this area.

By the end of the third grade the children are ready to start lessons in English. Pronunciation of English words is very hard for the Pitjantjatjara because English has many more sounds than their own tongue, which has only thirty-three. When the children practice their English they have to be reminded to talk more slowly and in a louder voice. Because they are so unsure of their pronunciation, they speak very softly. But though the children are self-conscious about their English, they don't want to go back to learning in the Pitjantjatjara tongue, though they will always be able to speak it. But they realize how important it is to learn English, which is spoken everywhere outside their tiny reserve.

A teacher with her class of Aboriginal students at the Indulkina reserve school. The child at the front desk, left, is the son of one of the school's Caucasian teachers.

Once a week the boys are given a workshop class where they are taught how to repair cars and other machinery. One day they will be able to take over the settlement garage, which is now being run by a white man.

The girls study home economics. They learn how to cook European dishes and how to sew, using a sewing machine.

The school curriculum includes math, English, and social studies. The teacher never singles out a child for individual praise. Aboriginal children don't like to compete with one another and those who are praised individually become so embarrassed that they slip back to the level of the others. The teacher must praise or criticize the whole class at once. But if some children do exceptional work they may get a word of encouragement whispered in their ears so softly none of the others can hear.

The Indulkina school, which is only a grammar school, starts the day with a video tape segment of Sesame Street shown in the school auditorium. It is a big attraction, bringing mothers and their preschool children in from the settlement to watch.

Afterward the mothers and babies leave. And the students go to their separate classes. No one pays much attention to their ages, which range from seven to seventeen. No one makes fun of an older student studying with younger ones. Only the desire for an education counts.

The children's teachers are white, but each teacher has an Aboriginal aide. The aides may have little schooling, but can help bridge the gap between the two cultures, explaining the teacher to the pupils and the pupils to the teacher. After school the teachers

Indulkina reserve Aboriginal school children working on their lessons in the schoolhouse. The Aboriginal woman in the foreground is a teacher's aide.

give courses to the aides to increase their education. Many of the aides are as eager as the pupils to improve their English.

Indulkina has a hospital, which is housed in a large, airy building with fully equipped examination rooms and medical supplies. The hospital is staffed by nurses. There is a maternity ward where they can deliver babies. Three Aboriginal aides help and also act as interpreters.

Once a month a doctor and nurse from the Alice Springs Public Health Service fly in to examine the more serious cases. The chief health problems among Aborigines are respiratory ones. Though some also suffer from eye diseases.

The nurses make periodic visits to the school to give lessons in simple hygiene. They teach the children how to use the toilet and flush it afterward and how to wash their hands properly. They also check eyes, ears, chests, and throats. They give immunization shots for such diseases as tetanus, typhoid, diphtheria, and measles. If they detect any suspicious symptoms during these checkups, they ask the child to come to the hospital after school for a further examination and perhaps treatment.

The Northern Territory Medical Service sends a plane and medical team periodically to check station people and the Aboriginal settlement hospital at Indulkina. The doctor, left, is from the United States. The nurse's aide who has come with him is between the young boy and his mother.

The People of Indulkina don't want their children to forget their own culture while learning the ways of Those Others. So periodically an old bush woman who knows all the secrets of this arid land takes the girls out on long jaunts to show them where to find the hidden edible foods that sustained their people through so many centuries.

A woman versed in the Aboriginal manner of spinning teaches the girls how to use crossed sticks for a spindle and how to roll the sheep's wool on their thighs to make yarn. In the early days the women spun human hair and then wove it into head pads, which they wore while carrying heavy loads.

An experienced bushman teaches the boys how to track and hunt. Today government subsidies enable The People to buy needed supplies from the little settlement shop. But on weekends they still go hunting for their traditional fare of kangaroo. They bag rabbits and goannas. With the women bringing in witchetty grubs and honey ants and other desert delicacies, there can be a big communal feast.

The boys are also taught how to use the spear and boomerang and how to carve them. As they grow older they are gradually prepared for the great initiation that still takes place in their teens and marks their passage from boyhood to adult life. Then they will be able to participate in the secret ritual conclaves the Aboriginal men still hold.

Periodically the teachers take their pupils on two-week outings to cities or the seacoast. One year the older boys go with their white teacher and two Aboriginal aides to Mornington Island lying in the Gulf of Carpentaria off the northern coast of Australia some 800 miles away. Mornington is the home of another tribe of Aborigines.

The bus of schoolchildren rolls through familiar territory at first. But as it continues northward the scenery changes and the Red Center gives way to a greener land. Here rainfall is heavier and there are many more trees. Some of them are varieties the boys have never seen before. One has a huge trunk in which it stores water for the dry season. It is the baobab tree. Tall slabs of termite hills five feet high dot the landscape looking like miniature yellow peaks.

In the summer everything will be drenched in torrential downpours. Swollen rivers will overflow their banks and flood the land. Now it is still the dry season and travel is easy.

Finally they reach the little fishing port of Karumba. It lies in the estuary of the Norman River that empties into the Gulf of Carpentaria. Here the boys board a small plane that is waiting to take them to Mornington Island.

Most of them are terrified as the plane rises, leaving the solid ground behind and soaring out over the sparkling seas. Even the

Aboriginal aides are gripping their seat arms, staring grimly ahead. Only the teacher is relaxed. And suddenly the boys feel easier.

In a very short while they are landing on the island and are being greeted by their hosts. They set up camp and for the next ten days learn what it is like to live on the ocean and get their food from it. Their hosts, who are adept fishermen, teach them how to spear the great fish or to catch them with line and bait. In the evenings they gather around the camp fires discussing the doings of their tribes, exchanging yarns, having singsongs, and playing games together.

This island set in a sparkling, throbbing sea of waters is a far cry from the great, red inland sea of land from which it is separated by so many miles. There water is so scarce it has always been the Pitjantjatjaras' greatest treasure.

The tossing, fluid ocean seems threatening to the Aboriginal chaperons. With every passing day they grow more and more homesick for the familiar landscape of their people. They are glad when the time arrives to return.

But the boys are sorry to leave. For months to come they will talk about this adventure as they sit around the camp fires in Indulkina. Each treasured incident, no matter how small, will be dredged up lovingly from the well of memory and shared with The People.

5

THE LESTERS
OF MIMILLEE STATION

Rosemary and Leroy Lester out for a Saturday canter.

In the low Everard Ranges some sixty miles from Indulkina stands the rambling homestead where Leroy, Rosemary, and Karina Lester live with their parents. The station, which is known as the Mimillee Cattle Company, is owned by the Yangkuntjatjara tribe of Aborigines, who for centuries have made their home in these ranges.

When the strangers from overseas arrived a half century ago, they turned the ranges into first a sheep and then a cattle station. And a homestead went up at Mimillee. Eventually Mimillee became part of Granite Downs Station. Then in 1972 the Federal Department for Aboriginal Affairs bought the thousand-square-mile Mimillee section with its forty-five hundred head of cattle and turned everything over to the Yangkuntjatjara people, to whom the land had belonged in the first place.

At first the government found white managers to help the Yang-kuntjatjara run the station. The managers knew all about cattle, but they and the Yangkuntjatjara could not get along because neither understood the language or ways of the other. So the Aboriginal council that runs Mimillee decided to pick their own man. They chose Jim Lester, a member of the Yangkuntjatjara tribe. Lester, who has both white and Aboriginal blood, was then working as an interpreter at the Aboriginal Development Institute in Alice Springs.

Lester could not believe the council's decision. After all he not only knew nothing about cattle, but he was also totally blind. But the council insisted.

"Here are Yangkuntjatjara men who have worked on cattle stations all their lives, they can help you with that end of it," they explained. "What we need is someone of our tribe who can speak English and who understands the ways of the white man to take care of the business end."

Jim talked it over with his wife, Lucy, who was born near Erna-bella and is a member of the Pitjantjatjara tribe. After long discussions they decided that Jim should at least try it. So in 1975 the Lesters with their three children moved to the rambling homestead in the heart of the Everards. After many years Jim Lester had returned at last to his boyhood home.

The Lester children know the story of their father's life for they have heard it many times. When he was very young he began losing his eyesight. And by 1957, when he was sixteen, he was almost totally blind. He was sent to a hospital in Adelaide to see if his eyes could be cured.

It was a terrifying experience for the young boy who had spent all his life in the open. Now he found himself imprisoned by four walls, unable to talk to anyone since he knew no English and nobody around him could speak the Yangkuntjatjara tongue. He could not even ask someone to contact his parents and tell them where he was. None of his tribe knew where he had gone. He had just disappeared as though off the face of the earth. Young Jim spent five weeks in the hospital while doctors worked to restore his sight, but they could do nothing. Since he was now totally blind and unable to care for himself it was impossible to send him back. So he was placed in a home for blind children in the Adelaide Hills.

Fortunately he met another blind Yangkuntjatjara there. This young man could speak English as well as his native tongue. The two became fast friends, and Jim decided that if he had to stay in the city he should learn to speak English too. He asked his friend to teach him. At the same time he began attending an institute for the blind to learn a trade—making brooms—so that he could support himself.

In 1966 Jim married Lucy, whom he had met at the Royal Adelaide Hospital where she was doing volunteer work. After their marriage he was offered the job of interpreter at the Aboriginal Development Institute in Alice Springs. He took his job seriously, remembering how desperate he had felt when he had been unable to explain his needs or talk about his fears. It was his patience and compassion that so impressed the council at Mimillee.

In the following years Jim learned a great deal about cattle and their needs, about bores and fences that had to be kept mended, and about machinery that broke down and had to be repaired. He knows now about mustering, drafting out the fats, ordering trucks to haul them away, booking cattle cars to take them to the city. He knows to check the markets before selling to be sure the prices are right.

In his small business office equipped with a transceiver set, he can handle much of the business by voice or telegram. Lucy helps by taking care of accounts, writing letters, and drawing up schedules. She is prepared to drive him anywhere he has to go.

The children help too. They fetch and carry for their father and serve as guides. With a hand on the shoulder of eleven-year-old Leroy or eight-year-old Rosemary or four-year-old Karina, he can get around the house and cattle yards and even walk over rough ground to the little settlement of Mimillee, which lies about a mile and a half from the homestead.

Besides helping her husband, Lucy has her own crowded schedule. Beds must be made, breakfast cooked, dishes washed, clothes ironed, chicks fed, eggs gathered. She also entertains visitors from Mimillee and other settlements, or, sometimes, government officials from the city.

At nine o'clock she sees that the children are in their classroom ready for their lessons. Though there is a little caravan school at Mimillee, Lucy is so busy around the house that she does not have time to take the children back and forth. So she has enrolled them in School of the Air. Leroy is in the sixth grade and Rosemary is in the third.

Their schoolroom is neat and gay with bright new curtains at the windows. Here the children do their homework faithfully under the supervision of a young girl from Adelaide who is their governess.

Lucy knows how important a good education is if her children are to fit into the modern world, so nothing is allowed to interfere with their schooling. They aren't even given the day off when a big convention of Aboriginal tribes is held at Mimillee. Some two hundred Aborigines gather from this area of Australia. Camping out around the little settlement, they spend two days in an open-air convention, discussing their problems and the possible solutions for them.

Lucy and the other Mimillee women are kept busy serving food to their guests. The community kitchen is a large open-air shelter called a tucker wurley. It stands near the meeting place. The women barbeque steaks in the shed and serve them with bread or scones. A blazing fire laid under a half drum perched on four legs provides boiling water for tea and coffee.

Karina guides her father to the meetings and helps him find his way around. But the older children and their governess stay behind in the station house poring over their books.

Left: Little Karina Lester sits in her playhouse with her pet dog. Brush stacked on top of a framework of timber acts as shelter against the sun in this modern version of the Aborigine wurley.
Right: Lucy Lester has interested the women of Mimillee in establishing a handicraft center where they can make such popular tourist items as the hand-painted skirt she is wearing.

The women of Mimillee enjoy taking an active part in community doings. They have so much time on their hands that they and Lucy are talking about starting a handicraft center like the one in Ernabella, which makes hand-printed materials to sell to tourists.

It takes money to start such a center and the women are slowly saving for it. They get secondhand clothing from the city and sell it at the settlements. Gradually they are building up their bank account. When they have enough to purchase supplies they will raise a simple shelter of spinifex to serve as their workshop until they can afford something better. Lucy, who spent part of her life at Ernabella, can show the women how to do the work. Perhaps an Ernabella woman will come to give them some training also.

On Saturdays, Rosemary and Leroy go riding. Their horses are brumbies—wild horses that the station hands have caught and broken in. Their father helps them saddle up. He hoists the heavy saddles on his shoulder and the children guide him to the corral where the horses are tethered. When they reach it he pulls out the heavy bar and Leroy swings the gate open. Then Rosemary leads their father to the horses.

The rest is simple for him. Feeling along the flanks of Rosemary's horse with practiced hands, he throws her saddle over its back. He adjusts it carefully and then bridles up. And Rosemary clambers on. Next Leroy's horse is saddled and bridled in the same manner.

The children take their father's skill for granted. They have seen him doing this so many times that they do not stop to think of how capable he is. They accept the reins from his hands as he unties them. Then he calls to Karina who is waiting at the gate. She comes obediently to lead her father back to the house and his work.

As the older children ride from the corral, their mother steps outside to call a word of warning: "Don't go far. Be careful."

She worries about the children when they are gone. If the horses are spooked and rear, they could be thrown and hurt. And there are always the snakes to think about. They come in numbers when the weather turns warm. Australia is the home of some of the deadliest snakes in the world. Just the previous year a Mimillee child was bitten by one and died before the Flying Doctors could arrive to take him to the hospital.

When the children return they comb and brush the horses down. Sometimes they trim the manes that hang over their eyes. They also clip their long, sweeping tails to keep the grass from catching in them, spooking them and making them buck.

The children have other chores too. They help with the dishes and the housecleaning and feed the chickens. Even Karina does her share, gathering the eggs and bringing them in for her mother. Now and then she cooks some for herself.

During holidays the older children like to go mustering at the stock camp where their father acts both as general adviser and camp cook. Sometimes the whole family goes out to check the bores. There are nineteen of these, and if Jim finds any that are not working he gets in touch with the station mechanic and discusses the problem with him. It is hoped that the bore can be patched without too much expense. Otherwise new parts will have to be ordered. But ordering too many new parts puts a strain on the company finances.

Often, before they set out on their tours of inspection, Lucy makes a lunch. After checking the bores the family stops for a picnic. One of their favorite places is on the banks of a large creek that flows only after a heavy rainfall. But the water holes scattered along its bed are fed by underground springs and are always full.

Cattle drink at the lower pools. In the higher reaches, however, the pools are unmuddied, clean, and sweet, and the children like to swim in them. Afterward they lie on the warm rocks and watch the wilderness life flow around them. Rabbits scurry in the undergrowth, lizards bask in the warm sun. Birds come to drink—swarms

Left: It's Leroy Lester's chore this morning to feed the chickens in the Lester coop at Mimillee Station. Many of the Outback stations keep their own fowl to ensure a steady supply of fresh eggs.
Right: Water tanks outside the cluster of houses at Mimillee station. They are a necessity at all Outback stations.

of green parakeets, delicate lorikeets, gray-and-rose galahs, black-and-white magpies, saucy willy-wagtails.

But the Everards are not always a friendly place. In these ranges summer thunderstorms can break with sudden ferocity. Lightning like jagged spears zigzags down, followed by crashing thunder.

Occasionally the lightning strikes and splits one of the huge mountain eucalypts. A shower of ruddy chips flies through the air starting small brush fires everywhere. The people of Mimillee rush out with buckets of water and shovels. They beat and stamp on the little patches of flame and drench them with water before they can gain strength.

One day a gigantic dust storm hurls itself upon the ranges. It begins as a strange black cloud lying along the horizon. Quickly the distant cloud comes boiling up into the sky borne on a fierce wind, which fills the whole world with its howling.

Blacker and blacker, nearer and nearer draws the whirling, roaring cloud. It is made up entirely of dust that the wind has scoured from the great red plains below.

As the cloud advances, mothers run screaming for their children, who are scattered everywhere at play. The shrieks of the women are caught and strangled by the wind. But the children are already rushing terrified to the little sheds that are their homes.

The wind hurls itself against a giant pepper tree, sending it crashing to the ground. It bends the tall eucalypts double, brushing their tops like giant brooms back and forth across the ground. A noisy tattoo sounds as one of the trees near the house begins to scrape across the roof.

Lucy worries that the flimsy shed down the road where a mother and her three children are sheltering will tip over and blow away. She rushes out to bring them to safety in the station house. Rosemary tries to follow but the wind rushes against her with such force that she is almost hurled from her feet.

"Go back," her mother shouts. "Shut the door." Leroy has to help her do it.

Rosemary watches her mother from the window. Bent double against the wind she is making her way to the shed. Soon she is swallowed up in the whirling dust. Even the nearby garage disappears from sight.

It seems a long while before Rosemary sees her mother returning, herding the terrified family before her. By the time they get into the house the world outside has become dark as night. The house itself is filled with a stifling blackness. Lucy turns on the electric lights. Then lightning zigzags through the black dust cloud, followed instantly by a deafening thunderclap. The lightning has struck very close.

Jim sends Leroy to turn off the generator for fear lightning will strike it and set the house afire. Lucy and Rosemary begin lighting candles and putting them around the table. Karina, screaming with fear, clings to her mother's skirts and the three children from down the way huddle with their mother in a corner.

Then drenching rains pour down and the howling wind fades. In an hour the rain stops and the sun is sparkling everywhere. But the storm has left a red havoc behind. The once green lawn is covered with a layer of red mud. There are muddy puddles in the house where wind and rain have forced their way through chinks and crevices. It will take hours to get the house clean again.

Rosemary is still haunted by the memory of the terrible thunderstorm. Sometimes when the wind howls around the house at night, she wakes up crying from a nightmare.

Then her father comes, feeling his way down the long corridor to her bedroom. He takes her in his arms and holds her until she quiets. Groping his way back he carries her with him to the room he shares with her mother.

Rosemary, her head against his shoulder, thinks of that blind boy of long ago lying in a hospital bed all alone in the dark. And she is comforted knowing how well he understands her loneliness and fear.

6

ABORIGINAL CHILDREN

Two Aboriginal schoolgirls, whose wistful, appealing faces are characteristic of all Aboriginal children. Once you have won their confidence they will shower you with affection.

Not all the Aboriginal children of central Australia are in settlements such as Indulkina and Ernabella and Mimillee. Some live in small towns. Others are scattered about on stations where their parents are employed. But wherever they may be, these children are the true heirs of the Outback. Their heritage is millennia of living in harmony with the great tawny wilderness.

The land holds few secrets from them. Almost from birth their eyes are sharpened to observe the faintest tracks, to read directions from sun and stars and wind. And so they are able to find their way home no matter how far away they may stray, and meanwhile they know how to sustain themselves on desert roots and plants and how to locate water. Their ears are alert for the softest sounds— the slithering of lizards or small desert animals or rabbits that, snared, might bring them food.

They live in close family groups that move with the slow rhythms of the desert. They have learned well the lesson of patience. And they find their excitement in a successful kangaroo hunt, the bagging of a goanna, or the discovery of witchetty grubs or honey ants. Put together with other desert fruits and nuts, they make a feast that food bought with government subsidies cannot equal in their eyes.

Left: These children show off the treasures they have dug up—witchetty grubs.
Right: An Aboriginal boy at Anna Creek Station proudly shows off his dog and nursing pups.

Both in the settlements and at the stations many of the older Aborigines still follow the ancient taboos and hold to the old beliefs. They continue to pay homage to their ancestral totem, whether it be an animal, a bird, a reptile, or a stone.

They have faith in the ability of the medicine man to cure. And when they fall ill they may call him in as well as the white doctor. He will conduct the age-old ritual over them during which he seems to remove the offending object—a stone, a twig—from the body of the sufferer. Often the psychological effect is so strong that the patient starts mending almost at once.

When despite the medicine man's ministrations a person dies mysteriously, the old people whisper of the bone-pointing magical curse laid upon him by an evil sorcerer. The medicine man may then be hired to find out the identity of the sorcerer and lay a recipro-cal curse on him so that the dead may be avenged.

The fear of ghosts is still strong among most Aborigines. This fear recently made itself evident at Anna Creek Station where a few Aborigines working for Richard Nunn live with their families in a small settlement on the hills. When a young ringer, only thirteen years old, was killed by a fall from his horse, the Nunns felt he should be buried on the grounds. After all, he had been born on the station and had spent all his young life there.

But the grave was apparently placed too close to the settlement for comfort. And people began whispering of leaving their houses. Things eventually settled down because the boy had not died in the settlement itself.

But then another even more serious crisis erupted. Two drunken women quarreled in one of the settlement houses and one stabbed the other to death with a knife. The Aborigines were sure that the house in which the woman was killed had been polluted. They even feared that the whole settlement may have been contaminated. They all left the houses and begin camping out in the dry creek bed. The whispers of deserting the settlement altogether now turned into open talk.

There was talk too of the dreadful Kurdaitcha man, the tribal executioner. Surely he would arrive presently to avenge the mur-dered woman. The children were almost wild with terror. They avoided the dark, scurrying for light and shelter. And sometimes wakening from sleep they cried out that they could hear the slithering footsteps of the Kurdaitcha in the gusts of wind that rush ghostlike over the plains. One morning six-year-old Johnny burst into the station's small school house, his eyes popping with terror.

"I saw the Kurdaitcha man last night," he cried. "Down in the creek. He was there in his feathered shoes, shaking his spear."

There was that in the child's voice that almost convinced his white teacher, Steve Marshall. Marshall conducts grammar school classes in a little house built by the Nunns for this purpose. His salary comes from the government, and his pupils are all Aborigines. He must have at least eight of them to keep the school open. This is a problem because the parents move frequently, taking their children with them. Marshall considers it a great victory when nine-year-old David Jones elects to stay at Anna Creek Station to continue his schooling even though all his relatives have decided to move on.

Right now young David is interested in an education but things may change for him when he enters his teens. This is a very difficult time for Aboriginal children. As they become more and more exposed to the white world they begin to lose their beliefs in the old taboos and standards. They rebel against being ruled by their tribal elders who have lost much of their former authority but still cannot fit into the codes that govern the modern world. Often they drift into the cities and towns of the Outback. A few get some kind of employment here. Others, relying on government subsidies to support them, develop heavy drinking habits. Frequently their undisciplined behavior leads to violence and jail.

The tribal elders are concerned about the young people's growing alienation from the old ways of doing things. But few of these older men recognize the need to relax some of their rigid regulations. After all, they point out, these laws have brought their people safely through thousands of years. Surely they will serve them now.

Too often the youthful Aborigines become tragic, misunderstood figures living in a kind of no-man's-land between two cultures. However, the Department of Aboriginal Affairs of the Australian government is cooperating with politically oriented Aboriginal representatives to try to solve the problem. The answer, as they see it, lies in further education. This will help the young people in their dealings with the white world and give them greater self-confidence.

Since most of the settlement schools stop at the sixth grade the government offers scholarships to all Aboriginal children so that they can continue their studies. So far few have taken advantage of the scholarships. Those who do usually go to high schools special-izing in agriculture or animal husbandry. Such skills will be useful to them either in station or farm work or back on their settlements.

Some young people attend the boarding school for junior high and high school Aborigines that was opened in 1973 just outside Alice Springs. This is Yirara college, a coeducational institution serv-ing the tribal communities of central Australia. Qualifying children twelve years of age and over attend it.

Here English is taught as a second language. The boys are trained in such manual skills as welding and woodwork. The girls learn typing and cooking. The brightest students are given a thor-ough high school education. All receive lessons in the cultures of both the Aboriginal and European worlds so that they can make their own synthesis from the two sets of values.

Most of the Yirara students do well at their studies. The problem comes later. For the boys it starts when they reach fourteen years of age. Then they usually leave for the initiation rites conducted by their various tribes. Few of them return.

The girls tend to complete school. But then they also have to go back to their tribes. There they must again take up the restrictive life of an Aboriginal woman and perhaps follow tribal custom to marry an elder many years their senior. Under such circumstances there is no outlet for their newly acquired knowledge and skills.

To improve this situation the government is now arranging to hire the girls as teachers in their own communities. This not only gives them meaningful employment and with it independence, but enables them to help other Aboriginal children bridge the gap be-tween their traditional way of life and the modern world.

Some Aborigines are doing this successfully. They emerge as important political or professional figures, as creative artists, poets, authors. Their landscapes of the great red Outback are awash with color. Their vivid poems and stories of Aboriginal life and myths are giving modern civilization a better understanding of their people's ancient spiritual heritage and culture.

7

COMMONWEALTH HILL
SHEEP STATION

These two children, their father the manager of a sheep station, stand guard over sheep that have been mustered for shearing.

Even after cattle moved into the northern Outback, the southern Outback remained sheep country because sheep could fare better on the greater degree of brackish water and foliage that is found there. They thrive on saltbush, blue bush, and old man blue bush and on the wild clover, which in this area has a heavy salt content.

The chief problem in sheep country was the dingo. It could not do much harm to cattle, but sheep were an easy prey. So some seventy years ago a dog fence made of strong wire mesh was erected across Australia. It begins on the Great Australian Bight that lies off the continent's southern coast. From there it runs across South Australia and up through the center of Queensland in a great loop that ends in the sea. The dingo fence is some six thousand miles long. It is the longest fence in the world.

The government requires the graziers whose property fronts the fence to pay dog-fence rates. Every dollar is matched by two from the government. This money is used to buy wire mesh, posts, and other material. Each station is also granted an allowance to hire a man to do the repairs. The fence has been very effective in keeping the dingoes out of sheep country.

Biggest of the sheep properties that sprawl across South Australia is Commonwealth Hill, which is in fact the largest sheep property in the world. It is owned by B. H. MacLachlan. Mr. MacLachlan lives in Adelaide, leaving the running of the station to a manager. But he occasionally pays a visit to see how things are going.

Commonwealth Hill contains four thousand square miles of land. Rainfall is sparse here, averaging about six-and-a-half inches a year. But through careful management the property is able to run seventy thousand sheep, some twenty-six to the square mile.

Wherever water is located, bores are sunk and fences are put up enclosing forty-square-mile paddocks. The bores do not produce equal amounts of water. Some give only one hundred and fifty gallons an hour. From the larger bores water is piped to more distant paddocks. One big bore may water five hundred square miles of country through pipelines some forty miles long. This careful distribution of water has enabled Commonwealth Hill to support the large number of sheep it does.

The station is run by Mark Moore, who lives at the homestead with his wife and two daughters, seven-year-old Nicola and four-year-old Allison. Commonwealth Hill employs some twenty-three staff members, two of whom are overseers.

There are some twelve children living on the station. Most of the younger ones, including Nicola and Allison, attend School of the Air. Because they live in South Australia their school headquarters is at Port Augusta. Tricia and Sonia, teenage daughters of the station bookkeeper, are too old for School of the Air. They are taking high school correspondence courses.

The two girls have a part-time job on the station. Whenever

the cook gets a weekend off they take her place in the kitchen. They enjoy preparing the meals and they get some extra pocket money for it.

At Commonwealth Hill the year begins in November, the end of the Australian spring. Then rams and ewes are mated. Ordinarily female ewes and their lambs are kept in separate paddocks from those occupied by the rams. But in November, three rams are put in with every hundred ewes for breeding purposes. This is to make sure that all the lambs will be born just after shearing, which takes place in January—summer in Australia.

The time chosen for shearing is a matter of personal preference with graziers. Mark Moore chooses the summer. This enables the sheep to grow a good crop of wool by the time the winter cold sets in. Unless the sheep have thick coats, there is always the danger of losing some to frostbite.

Shearing time is the busiest season. The shearing teams are assembled by a contractor who rounds up jobs for itinerant workers at the various stations of the Outback. The team includes some six shearers and a classifier responsible for separating the shorn fleece into the right categories before it is baled and sent off to market. Then there is a cook and a rouseabout—a young unskilled worker who keeps floors and tables swept and handles the shorn fleece.

Two shearing sheds on Commonwealth Hill and two teams of shearers enable the shearing to be completed in six weeks instead of the three months it would take otherwise. Just before shearing time the shearers' quarters, empty the rest of the year, suddenly begin to bustle with life. The men pair off in the small rooms, which contain two beds each with mattresses and a chest of drawers. There are also adjacent shower and toilet blocks, a kitchen, and a dining hall.

Some of the men, however, prefer to bring their families with them. These drive caravan homes onto the station grounds and park them near the shearers' quarters. The wife of one of the shearers serves as cook for the men. Her two children play with those of the other shearers and with the children at the homestead.

Meanwhile the sheep are being mustered and brought into the yards near the shearing sheds. It is a simple process usually. The bore water is shut off so that the sheep have nothing to drink. Instead of wandering off to graze they cluster round the empty troughs expectantly. This makes it easier for station hands and jackeroos, using horses and motorbikes, to drive them into the yards.

Even then mustering sheep is not as simple a process as mustering cattle. If one sheep is allowed to wander off the others will start to follow it. Soon half the mob will be straying and will have to be rounded up again. So the musterers have to keep a lookout for sheep that seem about to break away from the others.

What a bustle there is on the first day of shearing! It begins very early in the morning because the sheep must be drafted and ready for the shearers, who start at half-past seven. The sheep are separated according to age and sex—rams, ewes, wethers, lambs. Each category produces wool of a different texture. It is easier for the classifier if the different types of fleece are kept separate from the beginning. Besides, the shearers prefer it that way.

The shed is a fascinating place for the children. They like to visit it and watch the shearers standing at their stations along one wall. Overhead an electric cord runs the length of the wall and is connected to a generator outside the shed. Electric shears are plugged into the cord and dangle beside each shearer.

On the other side of the wall are the pens with ramps leading up to low doorways cut in the wall. Beside each shearer there are two doorways, equipped with swinging doors. Through the first of the doorways the woolly sheep are hauled into the shed. After they are shorn they will be pushed out through the second doorway.

Now the motor is switched on and the sound of its throbbing and the hum of shears fill the shed. The shearers reach through their doors and pull out a sheep each. Quickly they set the sheep on its rump, holding it upright between their knees. Down go the

Above: Sheep being mustered for their annual shearing.
Center: A young woman station hand mustering sheep.
Below: Sheep are loaded onto a truck that will take them to the shearing shed.

shears over the sheep's belly, then down and over one hind leg, back to the neck and shoulders, down the two front legs, and down to the last hind leg. Now and then a shearer may make a nick when the cutter runs over a wrinkle. Sometimes the shears run into sand and dirt in the wool and become blunted. Then instead of clipping, the shears start pulling. This makes the sheep kick and squirm into the cutter on top of the comb, causing a deep gash in the flesh. When this happens the shearer has to take time out to stitch up the wound with the needle and thread handy on a shelf at his side.

Sheep are shorn in the shearing shed.

Usually it takes about three minutes to clip a sheep, the shorn fleece coming off all of a piece. While the shearer reaches for a second sheep the rouseabout picks up the shorn fleece and throws it on the large table in the center of the room. Here the dirty fringe, usually some six to eight inches deep, is torn off, or skirted as it is called. It is full of burrs picked up from the bindi-eye vines that sprawl over the plains of Australia. This fleece can only be sold as secondhand wool and will be used for such products as rugs.

After the fleece has been classified according to texture and quality, the baler scoops it up and either sets it aside or puts it in

Left: Shorn fleece is skirted—the dirty fringe, full of burrs, is ripped off.
Right: Fleece is baled preparatory to being shipped out.

the appropriate sack, which stands on giant scales. When the bale reaches a certain weight the baler removes it, seals it, and stencils it with the Commonwealth Hill trademark. Later it will be trucked off to be freighted by train into Adelaide.

There is no talk among the shearers as they work. They are paid by the piece and the amount they earn depends on their skill. Minor discomforts do not slow them down. They ignore their aching backs, caused by the constant stooped position they must take. The bindi-eye burrs are continually brushing off the wool and sticking into their hands. But they do not bother to remove them until the end of the day when often they have to use tweezers to get them out. Afterward they carefully cleanse their hands. Untreated the sores can become infected.

Around ten o'clock the shearers' cook, accompanied by her two children, arrives bringing the smoko treats to each shed—sandwiches, cakes, scones, tea, and coffee. The shearers relax. They joke with the children, tell yarns and tall stories about one another.

Laughter rings in the shed. Then the shearers get back to work and silence returns.

After the sheep have been shorn they are ready for dipping. The dip is a disinfectant that will treat their cuts and scrapes and also keep away blowflies. The great green flies lay their eggs wherever the skin is broken. The eggs hatch into larvae that gnaw out great chunks of flesh. The deep gouges become infected and eventually the sheep die of blood poisoning.

The disinfectant is called a dip because in the early days a tank filled with a disinfectant solution was used. The sheep were made to plunge into the tank and swim across it, thus immersing themselves in the water. Today the method is more efficient. The sheep are driven into a large cylinder in batches. Gates lock them in place and disinfectant sprays are turned on. The shower comes from all directions until the sheep are thoroughly wet.

They are released and the next batch takes its turn. After the sheep are sprayed they become lethargic, doughy as it is called in Australia. But they quickly recover, after which they are returned to their own paddocks.

Shorn sheep are sprayed with disinfectant in a process called dipping.

These shorn sheep are waiting to be returned to their pastures.

By the end of six weeks the excitement of shearing is over. The shearers leave along with their families and quiet descends on their vacated quarters. Then comes lambing time. This is followed by another six-week stretch of activity. The lambs' tails are cut off. Their ears are marked with the station identification. And the male lambs are castrated. Desexed male sheep are called wethers. They produce the best wool.

If there is a plague of blowflies in July and August, the sheep are crutched. In crutching, the wool is shorn off around the sheep's eyes and their tails, where the skin is especially moist. This exposes the eggs to the air, making it more difficult for them to survive.

The rest of the year is spent keeping equipment in repair and improving the land. Bores and windmills have to be constantly checked, pipes mended or replaced. Tanks that have corroded along the water line have to be coated with a thin lining of fiberglass.

Kangaroos are plentiful on Commonwealth Hill. Sometimes a wedge-tailed eagle soaring overhead swoops down to snatch up a lamb. But its chief food is rabbit. As pasturage springs up after heavy rains the rabbits multiply until they become a scourge, cropping the new grass down to the roots. At such times the eagle may even become a welcome predator.

8

STATION CHILDREN

Outback children are usually full as fun as are these two who live on a sheep station that their father and mother manage.

Only a few white people can find their way safely around the semi-desert vastnesses of the Outback. They prefer a nomadic life—going bush as it is called, the equivalent of the Aborigines' walkabout. Some of them earn a living as professional kangaroo shooters. When areas of the Outback become overpopulated with kangaroos the shooters are given permits to cull out the overpopulation, with strict orders not to shoot does with young. Kangaroo pelts are popular in some parts of the world. And kangaroo flesh is processed into pet food, so that the men are paid well for their game.

Other men, known as doggers, hunt the dingoes for the bounty the governments of the various states pay for them. Often Aborigines and whites team together in this venture because no white man can ferret out the dens of the dingoes as unerringly as the Aborigine. Then there are the rabbit hunters, both Aboriginal and white, who shoot and collect rabbits for sale in city markets.

But most of the white people of the Outback live either in little Outback towns or on stations. The lives of the station children circle around the nucleus of buildings that make up the station headquarters. Pinpointed in a platter of distances that stretches away horizonless around it, that cluster of houses is like a minute township in which the children have their own prominent niche.

Unlike the Aborigines most of the white children would probably not be able to find their way home if lost in the Outback. Mothers worry about this, constantly warning the younger ones to stick close to the homestead. When both parents go together to inspect and mend bores or to do some minor mustering, they take the children along.

As they grow old enough to venture out alone on motorbikes or in jeeps, the children are warned to follow certain rules. They must be sure they are carrying enough gas, or petrol as it is called in Australia. They must always tell someone where they are going and what track they intend to follow to get there. If their vehicle breaks down or get mired in a bog, they must wait beside it until someone comes along to rescue them. This will be a simple matter if they have not strayed from the course they have mapped out.

Grown people are given similar warnings. Those who fail to heed them seldom get another chance. Despite this, people are often careless.

One late spring afternoon the wife of a stockman wanders off from her disabled vehicle and becomes lost. A search is launched at once. Police are called in from Oodnadatta, a tiny town some seventy miles away. A search plane takes to the air. And a skilled tracker is brought in from Indulkina.

Hope seems to lie with the Aboriginal tracker. He finds the faint signs of her passing where others fail—a twig broken here and there along the way, a few bits of hair from the dog she has with her. By now the trail is two days old and the third day is passing by. Hour by hour the heat grows. A deathly stillness lies upon the baking sand dunes. Animals and lizards seek the shade of the mulga scrub.

Finally by late afternoon the tracker finds the woman. Her lips are blistered and she is dehydrated, but she is alive and conscious, though her dog is in a coma.

The woman was able to save herself only because she knew that cattle can be sustained for months without water by feeding on the lush parakilya plants. Because of the rare winter rains parakilya is growing everywhere and the woman has been chewing on mouthfuls of it. Fortunately for her a sudden heat wave has not yet burned the succulent plant away.

Left: Little Elaine Karger with some of the staff employed by her father, Terry Karger, at Orange Creek Station.
Right: The Campbell family, part Afghan (East Indian), part Aborigine, outside their cluster of houses at Orange Creek Station.

Marlyn and Terry Karger, who own Orange Creek Station, realize how important such knowledge can be in saving lives. And they are glad that their children, six-year-old Jonathan and four-year-old Elaine, have the companionship of Elaine, Tess, and Noreen Campbell. The Campbell girls, whose father and brothers work for the station, are a mixture of white, Aboriginal, and Afghan strains. But they have all the desert wisdom of their Aboriginal blood. No matter where the Campbell children may be, they can always find their way back to the homestead.

The Karger children often go out on excursions with the Campbells. From them they learn how to read directions by the position of the sun, the way the wind blows, the faint tracks of animals, men, or vehicles made in the dry earth. They learn what desert plants and berries and tubers can be safely eaten and how to find water in a seemingly arid expanse of plain. Marlyn Karger feels safer knowing her children have learned these valuable secrets.

The desert is a place of other dangers besides aridity and endless space. Warm days bring out poisonous snakes, which sometimes make their way into homesteads, even the children's bedrooms. There are scorpions, whose stings are quite venomous, and certain plants to be avoided. One is a tree from whose branches dangle tatters of what look like old black rags. The children learn never, never to stand in the shade of such trees no matter how hot the day. For the rags are actually nests of itchy grubs. If the nests are disturbed in any way, the grubs will scatter and fall, raising welts that cause swellings which may last for days and perhaps send the victim to a hospital.

But nature also has treasures that she reveals to the Outback children in ways city children seldom experience. When summer comes the Kargers like to sleep outside. Lying on their backs they stare up at the stars that, undimmed by city lights, sparkle so brightly. Jonathan and Elaine learn to pick out the Southern Cross, Orion, the Saucepan, and the Milky Way. Sometimes they follow the course of a United States satellite as it roves across the sky below the fixed stars.

Often on hot days their father teaches them how to predict a heat storm, watching it build up hour by hour from a little pocket-size cloud into towering white cumulus billows with black underbellies. When luminous white puffs begin to gather below, the children know that before too long a local storm will shake the world with lightning and thunder.

Among all their other chores the elder Kargers also find time to note and record the birds of their locality for the compilers of an upcoming *Guide to Australian Birds*. They identify the birds for their children—the little peewees so named for their call, the ringneck parrots, and the beautiful blue, yellow, and green princess parrots that add their splashes of gaudy color to the tawny land.

Farther south at Billa Kalina another bird-watcher, Peter Langdon, who is known in the Outback for his beautiful drawings of native birds, reveals the secrets of the button quail to his children. Breathlessly Katie and her brother watch the tiny mother bird only three inches long leading a procession of chicks no bigger than bits of fluff down a dry creek bed. The children also learn that the flocks of little orange-cheeked zebra finches which fly overhead morning and evening are on their way to water and that in the old days such flocks often acted as guides for thirsty Aborigines.

Maryanne and Debbie Young learn a different desert lore when they accompany their parents on a fence-mending trip. Their father Robin Young oversees the three-hundred-square-mile Mount Clarence Station, which is being used for the government's experimental projects. One of his chores is to check the sixty-five-mile length of dog fence that runs along the station boundary.

From the car the girls get glimpses of blue water surrounded by trees and cliffs lying on the far horizon. The scenes look real, but they are only mirages. Once long ago, their mother tells them, there was real water here, a great inland sea. Searching the desert floor the girls and their parents often find perfect mussel shells now turned to stone.

Along one section of fence their father shows them numbers of jagged stone tree stumps rising some two to three feet above the surrounding land. They are as big around as a large room. And their surfaces are plainly marked with rings that speak of the trees' great age.

Millions of years ago these trees must have crashed to earth all at one time, probably in a gigantic storm, their father explains.

The imprints they made when they fell show they must have been more than a hundred feet tall. The ground must have been soft mud then. The trees rotted away as the ground hardened, leaving empty shells behind. Here the girls can collect a store of treasure—splinters of petrified bark and wood that lie strewn around, relics of that mighty vanished forest.

Outback children have the usual collection of pets—dogs, cats, calves, horses, wild burros captured and tamed, wild rabbits trapped with lettuce or carrots, great white cockatoos. But there are also less conventional ones. They are the strange creatures of the Outback—frilly lizards, dragon lizards, blue-tongued lizards, sand toads that on dry days burrow into the sand and hibernate there until rain moistens the land. Sometimes it will be an eagle chick or a small kangaroo baby—joey as it is called in Australia—that has lost its mother to guns or cars.

Even when they are very young, children enjoy taking an active part in station life. Six-year-olds whose feet cannot reach the pedals

Left: Children of the Outback play games like children everywhere. These two are playing country store.
Right: When you're in the cattle yards, you'll get dust in your eyes. But no matter, that's part of the fun for these two Outback children.

proudly help with the muster by driving a light Toyota truck slowly after the cattle. In this flat land they can come to little harm. They also learn early how to do such things as change tires—useful knowledge when stranded with a flat miles from home. They develop independence and self-sufficiency at an early age.

The games they play are in mimicry of the life around them—mustering with the use of stick horses, storekeeping, and bore checking. But all these fade before the real-life events such as sheepshearing or cattle mustering. The children are caught up in the overall excitement and then School of the Air or even a visit to town loses appeal. Eight-year-old Rhonda Schmidt and her brother, Robbie, who live on a sheep station, appeal tearfully to their mother to be allowed to take part in the loading, shearing, and dipping of the sheep. Their mother, Lorna Schmidt, with the approval of the School of the Air, wisely gives the children respite from lessons during this time, with the understanding that they will make them up later.

As station children grow older their help becomes more and more important to their hard-pressed fathers. Most Outback people will tell you that the children are given chores to build character

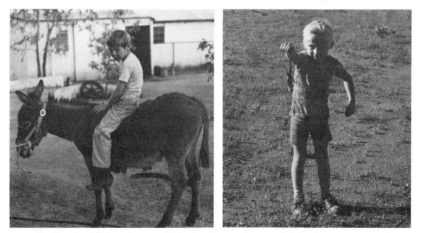

Outback children have all kinds of pets, from wild donkeys captured and tamed . . . to desert lizards.

and to train them in self-reliance, and this is doubtless true. But a few will admit that without their children's help they would be hard put to manage at times.

The young people feel a heady loyalty for their station and sometimes take on tasks that would tax an adult. One fourteen-year-old girl mustering sheep in a temperature of 125 degrees fell unconscious of sunstroke on the doorstep of her home. The story might have had a tragic ending if one of her parents had not returned in time to find her there.

When station children graduate from School of the Air at the age of twelve, most of them will go to Adelaide to continue their education. Some will be sent away to the city at an even earlier age.

School of the Air teachers at Port Augusta realize how hard it will be for these children to adjust to formal schooling in disciplined classrooms. So it has made arrangements with teachers and principals in an Adelaide grammar school to accept the Outback children as visitors whenever they come to the city with their parents.

Experiencing the routines of a regular school helps to lighten the shock the children feel when the time comes to attend such a school in earnest. But it is still a cruel wrench. For the first time they will be living away from the station for long periods. Some will be staying in private homes. But if they can afford it, Outback parents prefer sending their children to a boarding school where they know they will be carefully supervised.

Used to space, the teenagers suddenly find themselves confined to school grounds. Strict headmasters or headmistresses add to their sense of imprisonment. School of the Air has prepared them well academically, but they are not equipped socially to handle this new life. To Outback children, city people seem cold because they lack the hominess of station folk. Unused to competition they do not understand it among their schoolmates. And like Anna Nunn they suffer agonies of homesickness.

"We feel like misfits from the start," a boy explains. "We find out our cowboy boots and jackets which we wore on the station aren't right for the city."

A girl says, "Back on the station I didn't know anything about new fashions and my clothes were out-of-date. They made me stand out."

Outback children also become aware that their speech with its slight twang and colorful bush phrases is considered odd and a source of amusement by the sophisticated city children. Above all the newcomers find themselves excluded from an already established circle of school friends.

It takes long, painful months of adjustment before the Outback children are able to fit into their new surroundings and enjoy the novelty of school life. Even then vacation times and holidays when they can return home continue to shine in their lives like bright oases.

Once graduated from high school some of the children will return to station life. Others will go on to University. They may take up such professions as medicine, law or science, staying in the city to earn their livelihood. But always haunting them will be the wide reaches of the Outback, a memory that seems to grow more dear with time.

9

NATURAL DISASTERS

This is a water hole in a dry creek bed. Rains will turn the creek into a rushing torrent, but most of the time it is dry except for the water holes along its course.

Nowhere on earth is life governed more by weather than in the Outback, where rainfall averages only four to six inches a year. But monotonous months of sunshine can be broken at a moment's notice by violent cloudbursts as one or another section of the country receives an unexpected drenching.

Then dry creek beds flood their banks and nearby homesteads, forcing the occupants to higher ground where they may be marooned for days. Flash floods boiling down into dry, sunny areas may take unfortunate travelers by surprise, drowning them in a spate of wild water.

Heavy rains bring a halt to mustering, for horses and cattle and mechanical vehicles all become mired in a wilderness of red mud. The rain turns usually dry claypans into bogs. Such claypans are known as gilgais. A gilgai, which can be as large as a city block, holds water for two to three weeks longer than the plain around it. In its very center lies an opening called a crab hole where the ground has rotted away. The gilgai, sometimes overgrown with thick mulga grass, becomes a hidden bog where the unwary can be quickly mired.

Water in dry creek beds renews a poisonous weed called vervain. It attracts the horses but brings on blindness if they feed too heavily on it. Blindness is caused also by the poisonous paddymelon vines, which after a rainy season spread a coarse network over the ground and bear round, plum-sized fruit. The cattle will not touch it, but nothing will keep the horses away when it is in season.

Winds are a frequent occurrence. In the summer they blow almost continuously from September on into March. They keep the windmills turning, a cheap form of energy. But they are hot winds bringing sweltering days that are particularly dangerous for sheep. The animals become sluggish, searching out shady spots under the trees where they stretch out on one side. The fat congeals in the side next to the ground, stopping circulation. The side goes numb and the sheep is unable to get to its feet again without help. If it is not found in time it will lie there till it dies.

Lambing ewes often suffer the same fate. After giving birth they are unable to get up again and become easy prey for the ravenous crows that flock down and pick out their eyes blinding them. Then the birds are able to feed on the sheep at leisure. The defenseless lambs, unable to nurse, become prey to the eagles.

Sheep are not the only animals to suffer when heat engulfs the Outback. Birds drop dead out of the sky. Thousands flock to drink at the station tanks and many are not able to take wing again. During the record heat wave of 1979, Mark Moore, on his rides of inspection through Commonwealth Hill, saw hundreds of the pathetic green, red, pink-and-gray, and black feathered corpses floating on the top of the tank waters. Sometimes when a tap was turned on in the homestead, a melancholy feather would come drifting out.

Kangaroos in their desperate search for water began invading the tiny towns of the Outback. Many were dying of thirst. Cattle and sheep and rabbits were succumbing as well. During prolonged dry spells, as rabbits and other small animals die off, the dingoes become desperate. They are usually solitary hunters, but in lean times they may begin to run in pairs or even packs of five or six or more. Cattlemen claim the packs bedevil and distract cows to get their calves. Once the dingoes start running like this they continue to do so even when the need for it has passed.

The longest fence in the world is the Australian dog fence, which runs across most of Australia. It separates sheep country to the south, where the wild dingo can do the most damage, from cattle country to the north.

Because of the dog fence, dingoes cause few problems in sheep country. But their place is taken by domestic dogs, which if they become killers may be far more savage than the smaller, lighter dingo.

There are other hazards to the sheep. If hot weather is preceded by heavy rains, spear grass sprouts up everywhere lush and green, growing thick and tall as the season advances. At first it provides good fodder. But with the summer heat the spear grass begins to turn brittle. Presently its corkscrew seeds start to detach themselves and are scattered everywhere by the wind.

Each tiny seed is like an awl with crooked, hairlike arms. When the seed lands the arms twist round and round, driving it into the ground or any other surface. It forms cuffs around the sheep's ankles. The cuffs become so thick that they interlock, hobbling the animal's feet. Unable to walk it dies of starvation.

Dry spear grass is no longer good fodder. When the sheep graze on it the seeds lodge in their throats until their windpipes are completely blocked and they die.

Thick growths of four-foot-high spear grass also bring the danger of fire. Stretches of five-foot-high spinifex, and mulga grass growing waist high on the gilgais, add to the danger. An electrical storm striking with zigzag forks of lightning can easily start a blaze.

One such fire broke out on Commonwealth Hill in the summer of 1975. It began with a few small brush fires that were quickly fanned by the wind. Phalanxes of spear grass flared up in gouts of flame. The trees in creek beds and on sand hills, the stands of mulga—all went with an explosive *whush* as the fire hit them. Burning chips flew in every direction.

The fire soon formed a solid wall of flame that spread from Commonwealth Hill to Mabel Creek on the north and still farther. In this empty country there are few volunteers to try to contain the fire, which after all threatens no homes. So the fire fighters are mostly station hands and jackeroos from the stations. They set up a base camp near the fire front and from there went out with graders and trucks loaded with water tanks.

The graders carved a broad roadway four miles in front of the fire. Station hands carrying cans filled with diesel fuel and equipped with spouts walked along the inner margin of the firebreak waiting for the winds to turn. Then they set the grass alight on the inside of the break, hoping that before the winds shifted again the backfires would burn out the area, starving out the fire.

But the work was discouraging. At nightfall it would look as though everything was contained. Then the next day several little whirly winds would rise in the smoldering plain, snatch up swatches of burning grasses, and dance across the firebreak to drop their burdens on the brush beyond.

At the request of the South Australian fire department, Ian Rankin of Mabel Creek Station took up his light airplane to survey the extent of the fire. Mile after mile from Serpentine Lake at Commonwealth Hill he flew northward. As far as he could see, the bushfire was burning below, past his ranch, past Mount Clarence and Mount Willoughby, and on north into Granite Downs—a fire with a two-hundred-mile front.

From overhead Rankin looked down on bulls clustered in stunned groups around dams. Wild horses huddled tightly together in culs-de-sac. Kangaroos, dingoes, rabbits were all fleeing. Only the hawks still circled serenely about their business. As they spied the smaller animals drop, they would swoop down to clutch the tiny bodies in their sharp talons and soar away again.

Finally after some three weeks of burning, the winds died down, allowing the fires to smolder out. More than fifteen hundred square miles of Commonwealth Hill had been scorched. Many sheep had been burned to death. Others escaped the fire but died later when they started wandering back over the blistering ground in search of water. Then the heat cooked the thin protective shell that covers a sheep's hoof. When the shell sluffed off, the sheep were too crippled to walk and died of starvation. More than 2,000 were lost on Commonwealth Hill alone.

Losses of machinery as well as livestock were also great. Up on Mabel Creek Station, Rankin estimated that his broken-down machinery would cost him up to seven thousand dollars to replace. Commonwealth Hill suffered similarly.

Worse than flood or fire or summer heat is the ever-ominous threat of drought that hangs like doom over the whole Outback. Two years without rain is considered just a dry spell. As long as there is drinking water and the cattle and sheep can find a scant amount of herbiage, they will survive, though they may be reduced to skin and bone. But if the drought lasts longer stations are in trouble. The plain becomes a desolate platter from which the last

Low hills in the distance break the monotony of the plains, which give root to only sparse foliage at best. In protracted droughts even this sparse foliage dries and blows away.

of the herbiage has been eaten by desperate animals or else blown away by the winds.

Still vivid in everyone's memory is the Big Drought that began back in 1956 and lasted for ten years. During the Big Drought there were only two colors in the land—red plains and purple hill ranges. Not a single blade of grass raised a spear in that red-and-purple land. Even the trees shed their leaves. Whole groves of mulga died, leaving gnarled skeletons against the blazing cobalt sky.

Recalling the Big Drought one old-timer shakes his head and says, "The land was that empty you could drive a flea a hundred miles across it and never lose it."

The creatures in the Outback died by the thousands—cattle, sheep, horses, rabbits, dingoes, kangaroos, birds. Their bloated and stinking bodies ringed bores and water troughs. Whitened skeletons strewed the Outback wastes.

Furnace-hot winds created by the drought howled over the parched plains, blackening the sky with their great loads of dust. One day they would pick up whole rows of sand dunes and whirl them away to drop them farther on. Another day they would blow in the opposite direction, carrying the sand hills back with them.

Water troughs were clogged with dirt and had to be constantly cleaned out by weary station hands. Sand in drifts covered the green lawns of the homesteads and, despite tightly shut doors and windows, sifted inside. Every mouthful of drinking water and food was impregnated with it. Each day discouraged housewives had to shovel it out in bucketfuls.

Even with the help of government subsidies and generous bank loans, many owners were unable to carry the load any longer. They sold their properties for what they could get for them and left the land.

When finally the Big Drought broke, pastoralists in many parts of Australia counted their losses. Stations that had carried some 20,000 sheep were now down to 500. Stations of 5,500 cattle ended with only 350. Four thousand head on one station had dwindled to 96. And so the tragic roll call went.

But for those who hung on, the first drenching downpour was an unbelievable miracle. Parents rushed out into the storm to feel the rain cascade down upon them. They screamed and laughed and cried with hysterical joy, dancing in the mud, while their youngest children, who had never seen rain before, huddled on the veranda of the homestead shrieking in terror at the strange sight.

10

TRANSPORTATION

Two children walk on new railway tracks that seem to stretch on and on against the flat platter of plain.

In the days before railroads and trucks crossed the Outback, drovers used to walk the cattle—mobs of twelve hundred to three thousand head—over hundreds of miles to reach Darwin on the north coast or Adelaide on the south. Life was primitive for the drover. His tucker was salt-dried beef and damper.

For years damper was a staple in the Outback and is still eaten today. It is made of flour and water mixed to a stiff dough and then put in the camp oven, which is placed on top of a few coals. Ashes and other coals are set on top of it and the damper is allowed to cook for an hour. It comes out a hard, heavy bread.

Large-scale droving stopped when railroads and trucks were introduced to the Outback. Gold discovered at Kalgoorlie in Western Australia brought the Transcontinental Railway into being. It opened in 1917.

On its way from Port Augusta the train bypasses Woomera, for many years the base of secret-weapons research conducted by army personnel and scientists from Australia, the United Kingdom, and the United States. Recently the facility has been scaled down. But the nearby tracking station still plots the course of the United States satellites as they cross over South Australia.

The train's course takes it through the flat treeless wastes of the great Nullarbor Plain that stretches across Western Australia. It passes Kalgoorlie and finally, after almost a thousand miles, comes to an end at Perth on Australia's western coast. Here in 1979 the crippled United States Skylab plunged into the earth's atmosphere, traveling across the night sky like a brightly lit rocket. From there it strewed its burned-out rubble across miles of empty Outback.

During the early part of the train's course, it is bordered by a few sheep stations. Beyond them the land is uninhabited except for the small settlements that perch at infrequent intervals along the railway tracks. The settlements are called sidings in the Outback. And the men who live in them with their families are known as fettlers. A fettler is a railway maintenance man.

The fettlers are divided into teams that patrol the railway lines in section cars looking for loose bolts and other faults. Extremes of temperature sometimes expand and warp the rails, or they contract and snap the connecting bolts, breaking the rails. This damage has to be repaired immediately to prevent derailment.

Most of the sidings on the Transcontinental Railway are miles away from markets and shops. They are serviced by a slow train called the Tea and Sugar train because it carries tea and sugar and other necessities to the Outback people along its course. It makes a run every week from Port Augusta to Kalgoorlie, stopping at every siding. The train hauls an air-conditioned butcher's van; a grocery and household goods van; and water in rail tank wagons, which it delivers into the tanks that provide water for the little settlements.

The Tea and Sugar is the lifeline of the sidings. When its whistle

Above: A young couple who live on a siding consult with the Tea and Sugar train butcher.
Below: A small wayside store near a siding along the old railway that runs through cattle country.

blows, out flock the people bringing wheelbarrows, carts, prams, bags, boxes, and kerosene drums to haul off their week's purchases.

A second Outback railway connects Adelaide with Alice Springs. It was begun as early as 1880, but was not completed until 1929. For years cattle were freighted to market from sidings on this line. But it is in low country that is subject to frequent flooding. So the government has recently constructed a new line to the west of the old one. It has been more carefully surveyed and lies on higher ground.

Construction projects in the Outback bring newcomers who flock in like migratory birds. They stay long enough to do their work and then move on.

Neville Creek, his wife, Sharyn, and their seven-year-old son,

Jason, come in their huge Holden truck to which their caravan home is attached. Neville is a hauler traveling around Australia doing contract jobs. While the railway was being built, he helped carry crushed rocks to the construction site, where they were used for the bed along which the rails run. Sharyn made extra money cooking for the crew that came to mine the rock from a large quartzite hill rising out of the flat plains.

The Creeks love their nomad existence. Jason attended regular school for only one week when the family was in Adelaide, and he did not like it. He does not even care about missing School of the Air, which he can't make use of because his family moves around too much. Instead he takes correspondence courses, doing his lessons with help from his mother.

The little boy's companions are the chance creatures of the desert. One day he finds a half-dead pelican lying at the door of the caravan. He and his mother nurse it back to health. For several days it waddles after him. Then one morning it takes to the air in graceful flight. Jason knows he will never see it again.

Another time a black cat appears out of nowhere to join the Creeks. It is the descendant of a domestic cat gone wild and is much larger and more strongly muscled than the ordinary house cat. The feral cats, as they are called, are savage, ill-mannered hunters that have been responsible for wiping out much of Australia's rare native creatures. But Jason's new friend seems to prefer domestic life, drinking milk from a saucer and playing with the boy. One day, like the rest of his wild friends, it will slip quietly back into the broad, empty plains.

Jason's human relationships are just as casual. He gets to know and make friends with the crews with whom his father works. They show him such things as how rock is quarried and how the great machines are run that crush it into bits and then grade them. Jason knows that after the work is finished, he and the men must part, perhaps not to see one another again.

While the railroad was under construction a little mobile settlement accompanied its course northward to Alice Springs. The settlement contained large earth-moving equipment, caravans and prefabricated tin sheds, housing blocks of showers and toilets, two laundry rooms, a dining hall, and a recreation center. This was the temporary home of the construction crews and their families.

One caravan served as a school. The camp's nine older children attended it. Their teacher, John Jordan, had to handle four grades at once. His classroom was only thirty feet long by some ten feet wide. In winter the school was warmed by heaters. The days were frequently so cold that a rim of ice formed around the edges of puddles. And the children arrived muffled in layers of sweaters. Before they could start lessons they had to thaw out their fingers at the heaters.

Schoolchildren and their teacher (far left) in their mobile van schoolroom at the railway construction site.

By late spring, school had to be conducted in temperatures that sometimes soared to 102 degrees in the little caravan, which had only a fan to cool it. Swarms of flies buzzed in the stifling space. The students became short-tempered or lethargic. On those days Jordan let school out early.

Conditions at home also affected the children. Their families were an assorted lot. Some, like the Creeks, loved desert life. Others had left comfortable city homes because this job brought such high pay. But the wives felt lost in the great plains. Used to having a corner drugstore and a doctor's office nearby, they had nightmares of an emergency in which they would be cut off from immediate medical help.

Such women did not stay long, and when they left with the children they were usually soon followed by their homesick husbands. Then the company had to find new workers to take their places. There was a constant turnover before the track was completed.

Once the railway was opened, new settlements, adding to the sidings in the Outback, were established along its course. Manguri is one of these settlements. The houses that the government built and now rents to the fettlers at a low fee are modern and comfortable. But most of the six families who live here are not contented people. Some come from the city; others are footloose wanderers. Few remain longer than a year or two; some stay only months.

Old fettlers shake their heads and say it is not like bygone times when fettlers stayed on the job for years, especially on the line that crosses the Nullarbor plains from Port Augusta to Perth. Then there was plenty to occupy their time—large families for the

Mobile homes are a common sight in the Outback where itinerant workers and their families travel about searching for work. Note the prevalent water tank.

women to rear and a great deal of work for the men. The sidings had a community spirit. People went horseback riding and hunting together. They held parties up and down the line, with guests traveling by section cars to attend them. That is how the young people courted and married and stayed on.

Today such doings are only nostalgic memories, doubtless magnified and made golden by time. Modern families are small. New techniques of rail laying have cut repairs to a minimum. And in this modern world the slow rhythms of the past no longer satisfy. High pay and low rents scarcely make up for the long, empty hours that hang heavily on this generation of siding people. They cannot even while away their time with television, which so far has not penetrated much of the Outback.

Fewer than six children live in Manguri—not enough to open a school or even to get a government bus to take students to the one in Coober Pedy, the nearest town. Children can attend School of the Air, but the government does not provide siding people allowances for governesses. So mothers must supervise their children's lessons. But the women, who are often nervous and short-tempered, feel inadequate for the job.

Many give up and take their children back to the city. Their husbands follow them, or there are divorces and the husbands turn to drink. The women who stay often become depressed and emotionally ill and may start drinking too.

The Australian government recognizes the problems Outback women and their children face and has set up several programs to help them. Four times a year Infant Health Sisters travel into the Outback on the Tea and Sugar or by van to check the children's health. The Department of Railways provides the various sidings with motion picture films. Singing groups or threatrical troupes are encouraged to visit the sidings to give free performances.

The South Australian state government has set up its own program called RICE. The initials stand for Remote and Isolated Children's Exercises. The headquarters of the organization is in Port Augusta. Its purpose is to serve preschool children and their mothers whether on sidings or in stations.

The RICE team travels through the isolated areas of the Outback, visiting some two hundred and thirty families. One member of the team is a nurse who checks the children's health. If she finds any problems she discusses them with the child's mother and helps her make arrangements for medical help. Another member of the team is a social worker. She counsels with women who have emotional problems.

Lack of reading matter is a hardship for Outback families, so RICE brings a lending library of adult and children's books and toys. The books are loaned out one month and returned for new ones when RICE comes back the next month.

During every visit RICE handicraft teachers on the team conduct courses for both adults and children. Excited youngsters learn how to make all sorts of things out of waste scraps. The smallest children are soon laboriously weaving strips of brightly colored paper into mats or making themselves Indian headbands. The older ones are creating robots out of empty food containers.

Mothers are taught how to do such crafts as macrame, rug weaving, tatting, and knitting. Even men join the group. Spare time hangs less heavily on adults and children when there is something absorbing with which to fill long, boring hours.

11

THE CAMEL FARM

Camels serve as tucker wagon haulers in the flat wastes of Anna Creek, the only place in the Outback where camels are used in this way. Although slow, they are economical and efficient.

Alice Springs lies almost in the center of Australia. The little town is nestled among the purple Macdonnell ranges and is split by the Todd River, which flows only after rainfalls. But even in dry seasons the shallow bed still contains permanent water holes. And a little park has been built around them.

Aborigines, white people, and tourists rub shoulders in the small downtown area with its shops, restaurants, and motels. In the suburbs flowering trees line the streets. Rows of neat houses stand behind green lawns. Seasons of good rainfall are partly responsible for transforming the town from its former dusty Outback appearance. But it also relies heavily on water obtained from bores reaching down into the great subartesian basin that lies below it.

Some people worry about that water. Some bores that used to produce three thousand gallons an hour have fallen to one thousand. If the drop continues Alice Springs may one day return to the dusty anonymity of other Outback towns. Concerned scientists are studying the problem.

Alice Springs is the departure point for tourists going to Ayers Rock by bus. The sheer slopes of the sandstone monolith are a challenge to climbers.

Noel Fullerton's camel farm at Emily Gap, fifteen miles out of Alice Springs, is a different kind of attraction. People come here for a camel ride and a look at the small museum of camel lore nearby.

Fullerton has always been interested in camels and races them. When he first opened the farm he asked his old friend Gool Mahomet to come and help him with the camels. Mahomet is one of the last of the legendary camel drivers. He learned his skill from his father and has taught Fullerton's seven-year-old daughter, Alicia, how to make her own camel rise or kneel and how to guide it when she is riding. She has only to give a simple twitch to the rein that is attached to a peg inserted in the camel's nose and it

Left: Noel Fullerton (left), owner and trainer of the Alice Springs camel farm, Alicia Fullerton, his daughter, and Gool Mahomet, an old-time camel train guide who is now a trainer. When loads are to be carried long distances, the camel wears a wooden framework as pictured.
Right: Six-year-old Alicia Fullerton embraces her pet camel, Filmick.

will follow her direction as obediently as a well-trained horse. Unlike the horse the camel is a cud-chewing animal. It cannot be fitted with a bit because if it were to bring up its cud, the bit in its mouth could choke it to death.

"Treat your camel nicely," Uncle Gool warns Alicia, "or it will buck like a horse when you try to ride it—throw its head back and knock you off—or bite your leg. A camel can take a big chunk out of you, even crush your bones. I once saw a man who had half his face and his nose bitten off by a camel.

"But if you're kind you don't need to worry. A camel is the best mate a person can have."

The history of camels in Australia goes back more than a hundred years. The first ones were brought over in 1840. As they proved their worth in the trackless lands of the Red Center, more and more were imported. They all belonged to the one-hump species known as dromedaries.

Presently an Australian opened two stud farms and began raising his own camels. At the height of the camel era there were some twenty thousand camels in the country and twelve thousand were being used to haul produce, supplies, railroad equipment, building materials, and mail. Strings of seventy led by Afghans used to travel the Outback. Going twenty-five to thirty miles a day they would trek from Adelaide in the south to Darwin more than a thousand miles distant on the northern coast of Australia. Along the way they serviced the lonely homesteads, tiny settlements, and railway sidings springing up in the Outback.

No other animal could have survived those punishing treks over hot, barren lands where water holes were so few and herbiage so scarce. When the camels came across quantities of parakilya, copses of acacia and mulga, they grazed heartily. The excess food they ate was stored in their humps. When food was scarce they could draw on these supplies, which also provided moisture for their body tissues. This enabled them to go long periods without food or water.

As the camel used up its store of food, the hump shrank until the animal's back became almost as straight as that of a horse. When it reached this stage it was very close to death. But even then it could revive itself if it was given plenty of water. It could drink thirty gallons at a time and be back to normal within twelve hours.

The camel drivers, who were brought over from India and Afghanistan to handle the camels, had developed their own way of making saddles, which they introduced to Australia. The Afghan riding saddles have the seat in back of the hump instead of in front as with the Arab saddles. The pack saddles are topped with a framework of wood from which the loads can be suspended. The part that rests on the camel's back is covered with sacking stuffed with straw. All the saddles have a hole in the center so that the hump, which cannot bear weight of any kind, can protrude.

Since the camel humps were always changing size, the Afghans would spend their evenings around the camp fire making minor adjustments in the saddles. If the camels were feeding well they would remove a little of the straw stuffing. If the hump was shrinking they would stuff a little extra straw in to keep the saddle from chafing. The Afghans knew that an ill-fitting saddle could cause a festering sore that might take months to heal.

Loading was another art. A pair of Afghans would crouch down, one on either side of the camel. While one rested the five- to six-hundred-pound weight on his knees, the other tied the ropes in place. Then they would exchange routines. Every load had to be carefully adjusted so that it balanced. If this was done right a camel could carry anywhere from six hundred to twelve hundred pounds. But it had to be carefully helped to its feet, with an Afghan on either side to keep it steady.

During the trek the Afghans were careful not to make sudden moves because camels startle easily. If just one takes fright it can spook the whole train. Then camels may end in a tangled heap or race round and round in confused circles bucking saddles and loads as they go.

The Afghans were also careful to walk their camels over sand rather than stony ground. Camels' feet are soft and spongy. Walking long distances over stony surfaces damages the tender soles. Then the animal is laid up for nine months or more while it grows new soles.

As railways, better roads, and finally motorcars and trucks arrived in the Outback the camel became obsolete. The herds were released into the wilderness and the Afghans found other work.

The camels spread through the desert and semidesert regions of Australia. Today the continent has the only large herds of wild dromedaries in the world—some fifteen to eighteen thousand head. Many cattlemen look on the camels as pests because they knock down fences. They shoot them on sight. Sportsmen consider them fair game. Since there are no laws protecting camels, they are being killed in numbers.

But more and more people like the Fullertons are beginning to take an interest in the Australian camel, which is the only strain in the world that is completely disease free. There is a growing demand for them from foreign zoos. Arab countries are interested in purchasing them. Australians want trained camels for pets or racing.

As yet the Fullertons have not had time to breed enough camels to satisfy all these requests, so they have to depend on the wild-camel trappers for their supplies. The trappers usually find the camels in isolated, sandy country. When they spot a herd they approach it slowly and steadily on their motorbikes, nudging the animals toward their camp where temporary yards have been put up. Here trucks and several tame camels are waiting.

The tame camels help to quiet the fears of the wild ones. But sometimes a camel tries to run away. Then the trainer lassos it. As the camel starts bucking and jumping, the lassoer runs quickly round and round the animal winding the rope about its legs. When he pulls on the rope the camel is tripped and topples over.

Now the trapper fastens the two front legs of the camel together with hobble straps, then the two hind ones, and backs away. The camel sits up. It tries to stand but falls flat. Unless the trapper acts quickly the camel will die in this position because it cannot breathe properly. It must be forced to sit up again.

When the camel learns to stay in the seated position, the trapper removes the hobbles and ties the wild camel to a tame one. Once more he must move with speed and caution because when the camel realizes it is free, it may kick out even from the sitting position, sending the trapper sprawling.

The presence of the tame camel will finally quiet the wild one. It will settle down and follow docilely into the yard. From there the camels are loaded into trucks and carted off.

After the wild camels arrive at the camel farm, the work of training begins. Many of the same techniques used on the horse are applied to the camel. But the camel takes much longer to break

Barry Elliot, station hand on Bond Springs Station, and his pet camel, which he caught wild and has been training with hopes of one day entering a camel race. Barry was once employed as a camel train guide for tourists on jaunts across the Simpson desert.

in—anywhere from three to six months before it can be ridden without bucking.

Uncle Gool has many stories of the early days of camel life, and Alicia and her little sister, Michele, like to listen to them. As Uncle Gool talks he paints a vivid picture—the dark, wiry Afghans and their string of camels patiently plodding through the blazing day. The trek does not stop for a noon meal because it would be too hard to unload and load the camels again and too cruel to make them stand around under heavy burdens while the men eat and rest. So the Afghans keep going until the late afternoon. Then, moving among their animals, they settle them down and remove their heavy packs. But they leave the saddles in place until sunset because this is an old Afghan tradition. Meanwhile the camels are hobbled and bells are hung round their necks. Finally the saddles are removed and the animals are turned loose to graze while the men eat.

Through the old man's eyes the girls can watch the dusk deepen into sparkling nights of stars or moonlight. They can hear the distant howling of dingoes and the tinkling bells of the camels.

If any one of the camels breaks its hobbles and tries to stray, the Afghans will be up and after it, guided by the sound of the bell. If the men do not move quickly enough, the other camels will all try to follow, breaking their hobbles as they go. Then they may wander twenty to thirty miles away, and it will take half the next day to round them up again.

Wistfully Uncle Gool looks into the distance as he lives again in the long-past years. Then suddenly he stops talking to rub his aching knees. Almost every day for many years those knees had to support the heavy loads that were being fastened to the camels' backs.

"All that work, that lifting and holding," Uncle Gool mutters. "Don't feel it when you're young, girls. But when you get up the tree of life a little bit, then you do. Then you do."

12

THE OPAL MINES

In the opal fields surrounding Coober Pedy, mounds of excavated earth stand beside a shaft sunk by miners in their quest for the rare stone.

Midway down the Stuart Highway between Alice Springs and Port Augusta stands the little mining town of Coober Pedy. Coober Pedy is the English pronunciation of the Aboriginal word *kupa piti,* which anthropologists say means boys' water hole. They believe it was the former initiation site of a tribe of local Aborigines.

For miles around the little town there are heaps of golden earth, rising against the horizon like miniature pyramids or giant anthills. These are the diggings of the opal miners.

It is dangerous to walk in the fields because beside each heap there is an open shaft sinking some thirty to one hundred feet deep. Some of the shafts are still being worked. Others have been abandoned. None are covered and a step in any direction could plunge the unwary to serious injury or death. All have been sunk in a frantic search to discover the precious stone. Australia contains the largest opal fields in the world. And the land surrounding Coober Pedy is one of the richest of these fields.

Opal was formed as the great inland sea of Australia began to evaporate. Then the silica gel particles that were suspended in the water started to congeal and sink to the sea bottom. Here they worked their way into the thick sediment that covered the sandy floor of the ocean.

As the evaporation continued, new layers of sand settled on the silica gel deposits and new thin ribbons of silica settled on the sand. And so it went, layer after layer. Then the land on which the alternate layers were stacked started to crack and move. The liquid silica began to make its way into the newly formed cracks and crevices, slipping deeper and deeper down.

Today the liquid silica gel has hardened to form two kinds of opal. The colorless opal is known as potch. It is worthless. But in the potch thin ribbons of precious opal may sometimes be found. This true opal gets its color from the way in which the tiny spheres of silica gel have been packed together. They are stacked, like oranges in a crate, one on top of the other with tiny diamonds of space between each one. As the light beam passes through these spaces it refracts from the curved surfaces of the spheres. Since the spheres are at different levels they refract different wave lengths of light, each producing its own distinctive color. Among them the various wave lengths send back the seven colors of the spectrum.

The Coober Pedy opal field was discovered back in 1915 by a fourteen-year-old boy named Will Hutchison, who had come with his father and a prospecting team to look for gold in the area. For two years the fields could not be mined because they lay in barren, waterless plains where the average rainfall is less than four inches a year.

When the Transcontinental Railway opened in 1917, the fields were brought closer to civilization. And adventurers began coming with picks, shovels, and windlasses. They sank their shafts by hand and searched for traces of opal by candle or gaslight.

Once every two weeks camels hauled in mail and supplies from the railway lying one hundred and eighty miles to the south. When water was discovered some seventy-nine miles away it also came by camel. There was so little of it that it had to be rationed at twenty-five gallons a week per person. This was hardly enough for cooking and drinking. Bathing was forgotten.

In 1919 after the close of World War I, discharged soldiers began drifting to the opal fields seeking their fortunes. From their experiences in dugouts, so the story goes, they got the idea of making underground quarters for themselves. They equipped the tiny rooms with dilapidated beds and some kerosene cases for chairs. There was little else with which to build a house—no lumber on the treeless plain, no water to make adobe.

The underground rooms proved cool in summer, warm in winter, their temperature remaining in the comfortable 70s the year around. So everyone took to digging underground homes.

Today Coober Pedy's water problem has been solved with a giant desalinization plant, one of the largest in the Southern Hemisphere. A bore sunk some three hundred feet deep brings up salty water from the subartesian basin underlying Coober Pedy. The plant removes the salt and most of the twenty-eight trace minerals, some injurious to human beings, which the water contains. Two giant ionization towers rid it of its iron content. Now the town's supplies are ample, but water is expensive—twenty-eight dollars for every thousand gallons.

Water is brought to the homes by regular carriers who dump it into the tanks with which each home is equipped.

The town still has the dusty, gray look of its early days, unrelieved by greenery. A few low buildings line the street. There are snack bars, two supermarkets, a post office, a modern hospital, and a bank. The bank has such a dingy look no one would guess more money passes over its counter than does in most other South Australian banks.

Coober Pedy also has a modern hotel to take care of the people who like to come here on holidays to scratch through heaps of mining refuse in the hope of finding some overlooked opal chip. This is called noodling.

At the corner of a side street a group of Aborigines, surrounded by dogs of all sizes and colors, sit laughing and chatting. About two hundred Aborigines make their home in Coober Pedy. They live in a reserve on the fringes of town where they have their own mine and gift shop. Some of them earn from two to three thousand dollars a year noodling.

Coober Pedy's large, modern school stands in the center of town. It runs from primary through high school and has about five hundred students. Most of them go barefoot except in the coldest weather. The gritty sandstone dust that coats Coober Pedy has a way of working down between socks and skin and rubbing feet raw.

The school's headmaster, John Osborne, and his family are recent arrivals at Coober Pedy. They come from the Adelaide Hills. But the three Osborne children do not miss their old home. They find their new life strange and exciting.

Mike, the oldest, is thirteen and in the eighth grade. He does a little noodling. But he's more interested in playing football or basketball. He doesn't mind the dry, hot weather, or the willy-willies that whirl down the dirt streets in dusty processions around three or four every afternoon, or the swarming flies. He can always escape them in the underground home assigned the family by the Board of Education, which provides housing for teachers in country schools.

Coober Pedy is larger than it seems because most of the homes are dugouts. Only a few houses are visible above ground. Even the two churches in town are housed in spacious underground halls.

The Butts family home is carved into the side of one of the hills that fringe the town. It is a large place with nine huge rooms— three bedrooms, one bathroom, a spare room, a laundry room, a kitchen, a crafts room, and a living room. Len Butts dug it all out

Faye Butts, long time resident of Coober Pedy, works in her underground crafts room while her small son looks on. Her leather tooled goods are a favorite among her friends.

with a large tunneling machine, taking only three weeks to do it.

The Buttses' eight-year-old daughter, Ngarie, is in the third grade and their five-year-old son, Hayden, is in kindergarten. When Faye Butts came to Coober Pedy back in 1966, miners were still doing the work by hand. Her husband brought in the first large earth-moving equipment—big scrapers, bulldozers, and automatic augers. Later blowers were added to the assortment of modern machinery.

All this has made opal mining a lot quicker and easier. In ten to fifteen minutes an auger can burrow a ten-inch hole thirty feet deep. As the auger is brought up, carrying the loosened earth with it, the miners examine the material carefully. If it carries potch or traces of opal they will enlarge the hole and go down for a closer inspection. If they find what looks like a promising seam of opal, they will bring in a bulldozer and make a deep cut in the earth beside their shaft, pushing dirt up at either end. This is called an open cut.

At the level where the vein of opal is found, rippers attached to the bulldozer tear up the ground down the length of the cut. Behind the bulldozer come the miners carefully examining the disturbed earth for potch. If any is found it is checked for opal. If there is none the bulldozer pushes out the disturbed earth and again tears up the ground with the rippers. Once more the miner checks the loosened earth. If the bulldozer works its way down to one hundred feet without turning up any more traces of the precious stone, the project is abandoned.

Lately Coober Pedy miners have hit a slump. But two hundred and thirty miles north at Mintipi there are rumors of rich opal finds. And Len Butts has gone to try his luck there.

The Pivatos are more recent arrivals to Coober Pedy. Rosalind and Adriano Pivato with their two daughters, nine-year-old Melanie and seven-year-old Shevahn, also live in a dugout home. Rosalind Pivato comes from Scotland, her husband is an Italian. Some sixty-seven different nationalities are represented there in Coober Pedy,

The Pivatos live in this dugout home, which they bought ready-made.
Melanie and Shevahn Pivato survey the surrounding landscape of Coober Pedy from the top of the hill in which their home is dug.

including Greeks, Yugoslavs, Croatians, and Germans. Each nationality forms its own tightly knit social unit. Several have private clubs. The Pivatos belong to the Italian Club.

Adriano Pivato worked seventeen years in an Adelaide factory before he decided he had had enough of that kind of life and came to Coober Pedy to try his hand at opal mining. He had no experience, but he found a good partner—an older Italian who had been mining here for twenty-two years.

The two men obtained a permit from the Department of Mines and staked a claim simply by marking out a 164-foot square of land. Adriano and his partner sank a shaft in the center of the square and started looking for opal. Over the years the men have staked out a number of claims and sunk a series of shafts. Some have been losers. Others have shown enough promise to bring in the bulldozer for the open cut.

Once they find opal there are always buyers in Coober Pedy to purchase it from them. Most of the buyers are Chinese with their home base in Hong Kong. From Hong Kong they either export the opal to different markets around the world or they make jewelry with it.

On Saturdays Adriano takes his daughters down into his mine shaft for a visit. Melanie loves the deep, mysterious tunnel with its sheer walls stained in a mosaic of burnt red colors, over which the dim light of her father's pitman lamp plays. But Shevahn is more timid. She cannot bear to be too long away from the sun. And she is afraid that something will happen to her down there and she will never see the light of day again.

Adriano knows how she feels. After four years of mining he still shivers every time he goes down the shaft on the little board plank that is suspended at the end of a rope like a swing. People have sometimes fallen from these little swing chairs. Just recently a slab of loosened rock crushed one of his friends to death while he was in his tunnel. Sometimes fumes from the blasting overcome the miners. Blasting itself is a danger.

Left: Melanie (left) and Shevahn Pivato in their underground bedroom in the Pivato's dugout home. The design on the wall is the
natural strata of the hill's interior.
Right: Roz Pivato stands beside the open shaft of her husband
Adriano's test mine. The small board swing, raised and lowered
by means of the winch, is his sole means of descent and ascent.

Each blast has to be set off with a four-foot fuse, which takes
about three-and-a-half minutes from the time Adriano starts to light
it until it explodes. Adriano has to move like clockwork to get everything done on time—half a minute to light the fuse, half a minute
to get onto the seat, two-and-a-half minutes for his partner to pull
him out of harm's way. He knows that all is over with him if just
one thing goes wrong in that tight time schedule.

Adriano is a careful miner. He uses the more expensive gelignite
instead of the mixture of ammonium nitrate and diesel fuel, which
is cheaper and more powerful but easily set off. Even a charge of
static electricity will cause it to blow. Static electricity is generated
in many ways. Sometimes there is enough in a human body to
cause a blast. Nylon and dacron shirts, driving a car on a dry day,
an electrical storm can all build up static electricity. The danger is
so great that a sign outside the Coober Pedy drive-in theater warns

motorists against bringing dynamite in the trunks of their cars. NO DYNAMITE ALLOWED it reads.

Miners have safety rules. Wait a half hour after getting out of a car before working with explosives. Fix the charges underground where there is more humidity. Never work with explosives during an electrical storm.

But miners are often careless and accidents sometimes occur. Feet, hands, legs, arms, faces are blown off. Men have been killed outright by explosives set off by static electricity.

There are other dangers on the opal fields. Precious stones like precious metals inspire greed. And people learn to be tight-lipped about their finds. Rumors that a miner has struck it rich spread rapidly, bringing thieves to his mine or home. People have been murdered for opal as for gold.

Though Coober Pedy has many of the elements of a raw mining town, it has also developed a strong community spirit. This is the work of the growing numbers of women with families who have come to live here and want their town to be a safe and attractive place for their children. They have raised funds to provide tennis courts, a golf course, and a clubhouse. The well-equipped modern hospital is the result of their teamwork. Many are on its board. Currently the women are raising funds for the development of a giant new sports complex.

The Buttses and Adriano Pivato love Coober Pedy with its promise of adventure and instant success. To the children it is home. But sometimes Rosalind Pivato thinks longingly of green and lovely Adelaide, which reminds her so much of her old home in Edinburgh, Scotland.

13

HOLIDAYS
AND GET-TOGETHERS

These School of the Air children are singing Christmas carols at their Christmas performance. Each child has practiced over the two-way radio, but it is the first time they have all sung together.

The secret ritualistic dances of the Aboriginal men, which are still performed, are not for entertainment. But the different tribes do hold corroborees for everyone. Sometimes a convention of tribes may hold a joint corroboree.

The corroborees take place only after nightfall and usually follow a round of feasting. They are performed around the camp fires by the men while in the background the women will often sing softly with accompanying gestures.

In the north the dancing is punctuated by the hollow notes of the didjeridu. The didjeridu is made of a large hollow tree trunk or branch. It is four to five feet long, and its interior is hollowed to a two-inch diameter. When the player blows on it the didjeridu gives out a deep, booming sound.

Sometimes the rhythm is kept by women hitting their thighs with cupped hands. The rhythmic thumping and singing is broken with loud calls as the dancers announce the end of one movement and the beginning of the next.

The fires blaze up drawing out long, swaying shadows from the stamping, shouting dancers. Dust rises in rosy clouds. And children shriek with excitement.

The themes of the corroboree are simple ones. They may describe everyday experiences such as hunting the kangaroo, the rabbit, or the goanna. They may show the ways of birds and animals and men—how the kangaroo bounds, how the emu struts, how men hunt or play cards. In wild crescendos of sound they may mimic a great windstorm or a flash flood.

Some of the corroboree songs have been handed down through generations. They tell the stories of the legendary totemic heroes. Sometimes the tale may last through eight to ten nights with a new episode every night. Virgorously the young men strut and stamp to impress the young women in the audience.

Modern transportation in the Outback has enabled tribes from farther and farther away to gather in greater numbers for the corroborees. In 1978 one of the most unique of these corroborees was held in the Red Center near sacred Ayers Rock. It was made possible by air travel. Through their national Aboriginal council, the Aborigines invited the Maoris of New Zealand some three thousand miles across the ocean to the east to come to central Australia and take part in a giant corroboree. For more than a week Maoris and Aborigines displayed their ritual dances and songs, exchanged views, and made friends. The coming together of these two peoples from such great distances was an epochal event to be remembered for many years by both peoples.

But large entertainments of this kind do not come often to the Outback because distances are so great. At the stations the tight routines of livestock work don't allow for many social events.

A visitor to a station usually is treated to a barbecue dinner and an overnight stay.

Visiting in town is another rare social treat for white and Aborigine alike. The town may be Alice Springs or Coober Pedy or Port Augusta or any one of a number of tiny Outback places. More infrequently it will be Adelaide. If School of the Air students come to a town where their school is based, the highlight of the day will be a visit to it. Here they will be welcomed by principal and teachers. They will see their artwork displayed on the school bulletin board. If lessons are in session they may be allowed to broadcast greetings to their friends.

Parents, School of the Air, and RICE all try to bring the children together as often as possible. At the Parents Club meetings, which are held once a month over the transceiver sets, the mothers discuss methods of raising money to provide get-togethers and outings for their children.

This is difficult in Alice Springs because the children are scattered over especially wide areas. But the school does hold one get-together week in August. Then as many students as possible come into Alice Springs. They attend workshops in the school and end the week with a picnic sports meet at the little park on the Todd River. Children make new friends and indulge in scuffling matches. They discover that in the child's world if you hit someone you'll likely be hit back.

The Parents Club of the Port Augusta School of the Air arranges for an April outing. Then the children are taken to such interesting places as an ice-cream factory, a local school, a police barracks, or perhaps they'll attend a sports event.

A second get-together fostered by parents, School of the Air, and RICE takes place on the long three-day holiday that falls in October. It is usually held at a different station each year. One of the favorite places is Arcoona Sheep Station.

The Oads, who manage the station, turn over the vacant shearers' quarters to the children and their parents. The families sleep in the barracks, bathe in the block of shower stalls nearby, use the adjacent toilets, and have their meals in the shearers' kitchen.

The weekend is spent in organized games, handicraft workshops, and singsongs. Saturday ends with a big barbecue, the official close of the get-together, which has been as much fun for the parents as for the children.

Christmas is a highlight in the lives of the Outback people. One year Lucy Lester and the other women in the little Aboriginal settlement of Mimillee decide to give their children a Christmas party. Each woman contributes her share of money with which Lucy purchases candy, balloons, a tree, and decorations in Alice Springs.

For a week the women bake cakes and cookies—or biscuits (bickies) as they're called in Australia. The day before the party they hang balloons around the station house and decorate the tree. When the guests arrive, some sixty in all, Leroy, Rosemary, and

Left: At the Port Augusta School of the Air October (spring in the down-under land) get-together, children sit down for a songfest under the trees on the dunes.
Right: At Outback get-togethers, the children play competitive games such as races. Such games are new to most of these children who have grown up in isolation.

Karina Lester hurry to greet them. The children's eyes dance as they look around them. It is their first Christmas party.

The Alice Springs School of the Air holds a Christmas party which includes both the studio personnel and children from the cattle stations. Those who are too far away to make the trip sit by their radio transceiver sets. Each child has been mailed a small noisemaking gift. The children are told to open the gifts and use them. And now the airwaves are filled with a pounding, tooting, clacking, yelling uproar to welcome in Christmas.

At Port Augusta the celebration is held on December 12. This is the official closing date for summer vacation in South Australia. All the parents who can bring their children to the little town that stands on a quiet inlet of the sea.

The children are entertained with games and movies while the parents and teachers plan for the new school year, which starts in February in this part of Australia. Saturday night the children put on a performance in the school auditorium. For months they have been practicing Christmas carols separately over their transceiver sets. Now they sing them in unison. Skits rehearsed just that afternoon are acted out for an enthusiastic audience. Every number is applauded even though the singing may be somewhat off-key. And the timid voices of the performers, reciting for the first time in public, don't carry beyond the footlights.

Mothers serve the dinner. And afterward Santa Claus or Father Christmas, as he is generally known in Australia, sits beside the Christmas tree handing out gifts. There is one for every child.

The next day there's a big seashore picnic. Then children who live in dry Outback plains can revel in the calm expanse of water that stretches away from the red shore of the inlet.

The children who live on the railway sidings are not neglected by Father Christmas. All their names along with their age and sex are collected from each siding and station and sent to an Adelaide store where appropriate gifts are selected. Railway personnel wrap and label each gift. An extra supply will take care of the children whose names for some reason or another have been overlooked. None are neglected—an unthinkable offense.

It is the Tea and Sugar train that carries Father Christmas across the Nullarbor Plain. On ordinary days of the year he is Alf Harris, a railway official. But he has been acting Father Christmas on this line for nineteen years. At each stop the children come swarming to greet him, some with their parents, others spilling out of school buses.

"Father Christmas! Father Christmas!" they scream at the hot ruddy-faced man standing at the doorway of the van shouting, "Ho! Ho! Ho!" In his red suit and long, white beard he looks very uncomfortable. The temperature is soaring to 120 degrees.

To each child Father Christmas hands a gift along with a bag of candy and some cold drinks. For each child he has a special word and a hearty laugh. He knows them all. Many of the children who come to see him belong to young parents to whom he once handed out gifts years ago. They have married and stayed on at the sidings to take up the same kind of work their parents did.

Left: The School of the Air children meet Father Christmas in the Port Augusta assembly room. There's a gift for every child.
Right: This young boy has taken part with adults in periodic motorbike scramble races, a favorite sport among Australians.

Sports in the Outback mainly revolve around racing events. There are scramble races with motorbikes and camel races at which Noel Fullerton is a familiar figure. However, it is the gymkhanas that draw the greatest crowds. People will travel for miles to attend one.

Gymkhanas are race meets held by the combined stations of one area and run as benefit affairs for such charities as the Royal Flying Doctor Service. The little town of Kulgera, which stands on the Stuart Highway, has its own gymkhana grounds, which contain a racecourse, a large hall, a block of showers and toilets, and a tucker wurley where some of the women sell sandwiches and cold drinks.

Late Friday of the gymkhana weekend the trucks and cars begin arriving from the various stations. Everyone comes—managers, owners, their families, the station hands, jackeroos, jilleroos, governesses, mechanics, Aborigines, and whites. They all bring their horses, which have either been specially bred, or trained for the gymkhanas. On ordinary days the horses may be used for mustering, but at the race meets they are expected to prove their mettle.

As people spill out, horses are tethered and fed. Tents begin to rise. Swags, food supplies, and suitcases are unloaded amid a babble of voices. The hubbub grows as people hurry to and fro, greeting one another. Though many are neighbors they may not have seen each other for months. Children dart in and out looking for friends, some of whom they know only by voice over School of the Air.

At dusk camp fires blossom. There is the aroma of broiling steaks as people prepare their evening meals. Someone strums a guitar. Youthful voices are singing. Young station hands search out the governesses they may have met at the last gymkhana or look for new girls. It is late at night before silence falls on the mushrooms of tents.

On Saturday the gymkhana starts with all kinds of novelty races for the children. There are races in which the young entrants, their feet swaddled in sacks, lead their horses to the finish line. There's the game of musical chairs. Only it's played with horses from which the children must jump and find a chair every time the music stops. There's one straight racing event for every age group—the twelve to sixteens, the ten to twelves, and the ten unders. Each will do a two-furlong stretch.

The children's races are followed by adult contests. There are races for men, races for women, obstacle races, novelty races, and the main event—the great race that will reveal the swiftest horse and the best rider of this gymkhana.

The riders are dressed in colorful silks like the jockeys in the big-town races. But this is all for fun. Prizes may be anything from bean-bag chairs to electrical appliances. The trophy for the main race is a big silver cup. The winners of that cup are as proud as if they had been competing for honors in one of the big national races.

By the end of the day everyone is grimy with red dust. And now the shower stalls are noisy with splashing water and laughter and voices calling to one another. The tents too are bustling with preparations. The transformation is complete when finally the crowds stream out of the tents and head for the big hall.

The women are colorful in their best evening dresses, hair carefully groomed, boots exchanged for city shoes. The little girls are in party clothes. Even the boys are slicked up in denim pants and jackets. And the men who are usually seen in faded jeans and old shirts are now wearing slacks and coats and ties.

The people of the Outback have so little chance to dress up that they take advantage of every opportunity to look their best. But the formality doesn't go beyond appearances. This is a family affair. Children are as welcome as adults in the big hall, decorated for the event with green boughs and flowers from numerous station gardens.

A dance band brought down from Alice Springs begins to play. And the hall becomes a kaleidoscope of shifting colors as old and young whirl around it. Little girls dance with their grandfathers, grand-mothers with their grandsons, married couples, single couples, the elderly, the young. Round and round, in and out, slow waltzes and lively discotheque numbers.

On this night the children choose their own bedtime. As they grow sleepy they drift off to their tents to climb into their swags or just fall asleep curled up in a corner of the hall. The adults dance on—one, two, three o'clock—a magical night. They cling to the golden moments and the hardiest see in the dawn.

Sunday, the last day, is given over to camp draft races. Now the men show their skill at all the numerous feats required of cattle-men—cutting cattle out of a herd, lassoing them for branding, snatching off the surcingle from a steer in full flight. Then it is all over. As the afternoon grows late, trucks are reloaded. Tents come down. The hour for parting has come.

Station hands and governesses make empty promises to write and keep in touch. They know they may never see each other again, for the distances that separate them are too great for frequent visits. Meanwhile the station hands may drift away to other places. The governesses will soon leave their Outback schoolrooms, perhaps before the next gymkhana rolls around. Only rarely can a brief gym-khana romance ripen into something more.

Children too must say their good-byes to newfound friends. They learn early that the gymkhana with its fairy-tale atmosphere is a fleeting golden bubble on the broad, empty face of the Outback. They can only hope that the next time round the magic will still be there.

14

THE FUTURE

The Karger family accompanying government men who are pitting and seeding an experimental plot on their land. If the tough mitchell and buffalo grass take hold one problem with soil erosion will have been solved in these arid stretches scoured by wind.

A hundred years ago few settlers had any understanding or concern for the delicate ecology on which the Outback is balanced. In rainy seasons they overstocked the land with flocks of sheep and herds of cattle. When dry spells came the animals would overcrop, tearing up the shallow-rooted desert foliage in their desperate search for food.

In 1929 when one of Australia's worst droughts descended on sheep country, graziers began chopping down whole stands of mulga trees to feed their animals.

Mulga is one of Australia's unique plants, found nowhere else in the world. It is hard to propagate. During their first three or four years the acidity in the plants protects them from grazing animals. But other factors work against them. The mulga must have a succession of good seasons with plenty of moisture to enable them to survive to adulthood. This is seldom the case in regions that are prone to drought. And today there are treeless plains where once mulga flourished.

When the drought ended, the land itself had suffered mortal damage. Great sections, gleaned of all protective herbiage, had been turned into dust bowls or barren rock-strewn expanses—gibber plains as they are called. Only a succession of good seasons was able after many years to restore some of these ruined lands. Others were never able to make a comeback.

South Australia, which is overall the driest state in the continent, has suffered most severely from the rape of its Outback lands. Today an awakened government, backed by an increasing number of concerned citizens and conservationists, is taking an active interest in preserving the national heritage. Not only the mulga, but all trees on public lands are now protected by law and cannot be cut down without a permit.

Since the government still owns the land on which the stations are located it has the power to revoke any lease and shut down any station that does not abide by the rules it lays down. Jurisdiction lies with the Department of Lands. A branch of the department, the Pastoral Board, acts as liaison between the government and station owners.

The Pastoral Board makes firsthand inspections of each station and evaluates the number of cattle or sheep it can safely carry. The station owners are then advised of their quota. When drought diminishes the amount of feed available in any one area, the Pastoral Board can order the sale or destruction of excess animals to keep the ground from being overcropped.

The board also stands ready to give aid in times of hardship. It negotiates with the railways for lower freight charges and with banks for low-term interest loans. It recommends subsidies to enable desperate station owners to survive the bad years.

To improve the grazing capability of the land and to study its ecological balance more closely the government has established experimental stations such as the one at Mount Clarence. Pastoralists are encouraged to take part in various land-reclamation projects.

At Orange Creek, Terry Karger agrees to an experiment in dryland seeding. The Karger and Campbell children watch a huge pitting machine dig rows of shallow furrows across some eighty acres of the station's most arid land. As it goes, the machine drops minute seeds of Mitchell and buffalo grass in the furrows. Both these grasses are perennials with stronger, deeper roots than the desert annuals. Hopefully an initial heavy rainfall will fill the grooves with water and the seeds will germinate, catch hold, and spread a root system under the soil and a protective matting over it holding it in place. In dry weather the grass will die back, but it will not blow away. After every rain it will turn green again, providing good food for the cattle. If the experiment is successful the Kargers will pit the rest of their arid land, bit by bit as they have time. If the grass seeds prove a failure the men will come back to experiment with other species.

The National Parks and Wildlife Service is also concerned with the rare animal life that lives in the Outback. Many species have already become extinct because the hoofed animals introduced to the continent have beaten and firmed the once soft soil. Many tiny marsupial mice and kangaroo rats, unable to dig burrows in the hard ground, have succumbed to the blistering heat. Others have been slaughtered by feral cats and dogs.

But those animals that remain—among them the emu, the red plains kangaroo and the western gray kangaroo, the euro, the dingo, the wedge-tailed eagle, the many varieties of parrots and lizards— are all being studied. Most of the animals are now protected. Periodically department planes fly over the Outback taking a census of the red kangaroo, said to be gradually increasing in numbers since the wholesale slaughters of the past when twenty to twenty-two thousand kangaroos were shot yearly in a sixteen-mile radius alone. The increase has been due in part to the introduction of man-made watering places.

The arid Outback of central Australia does not encourage foreign investments as do the more prosperous stations to the north where rainfall is heavier. Alternating between drought and scanty rainfalls the less privileged of the Outback stations cannot predict profits or losses with any certainty. This makes it hard even to get bank loans.

Profits are also affected by the fluctuation of world prices. Let the prices go up but drought parch the land and the cattle will be too lean for market, the sheep unable to produce good wool. Let the cattle and sheep be in good condition but the world prices fall and sales will not pay for the freight into Adelaide.

There are also the spiraling costs of equipment, repairs, and supplies caused by inflation, coupled with the difficulty of finding good workers. In the early 1900s the young people who came to the stations loved the semihermit life and took the arduous conditions they found there for granted. They were men like old Bert Langley, who lives on a pension today, far from his children and grandchildren on Australia's green coastal fringe. Unable to tear himself away from the Outback, he has made his home in a small tin shed at the Anna Creek homestead. Here he swelters in summer, never dreaming of such comforts as air conditioners or even electric fans. He putters around the station vegetable garden, cooks his own meals, and sometimes invites a little Aboriginal girl who lives in the settlement on the hill to eat with him. It is on her that he lavishes his grandfatherly love.

Bert has few modern duplicates. Today many station owners are being forced to turn to unemployed city teenagers for their work force. Brought up on a television diet of glamorized station life—often of American origin—these young people sign up enthusiastically as jackeroos. They expect to enter a life of dashing motorcycle or horseback musterings, of songfests around camp fires and weekend parties where they can strike up a romance with some beautiful young station girl. Instead they find life a dull, dirty round of work with little amusement and low pay. Most of them don't last beyond four months. In the Outback they're known as mail-order cowboys—in one mail, back the next. Interestingly enough, in recent times more young women than young men are being drawn to station work.

What holds the station owner or manager to this hard life with its meager rewards? Perhaps it is the Australian dream that brings people like the Kargers, farmers from the green south, to the wild, beautiful stretches of Orange Creek—the haunting drum call of frontiers still to be won, personal freedoms to be enjoyed. Not freedom from work, no one expects that. But if one must be a slave let it be oneself who is the slave driver.

Today, however, more and more Australians outside the Outback feel this situation cannot continue indefinitely, and they speculate on what the future holds. Some suggest that it would be more efficient to cut down the size of the sprawling stations and fatten the cattle by grain feeding. Others speak of eliminating most stations altogether and turning the Outback into a tourist attraction.

Then there are those who dream of finding a cheap method of desalinizing the brackish bore water so that the fertile soil can be irrigated and turned into croplands. Others fear that this might dangerously deplete the underground water resources. Already some bores are drying up. Artesian and subartesian waters are falling back. Heavy irrigation also might draw salts and other minerals into the topsoil, turning it into an arid waste where nothing can grow.

However, hidden riches are being discovered in the Outback. Under some of these arid lands lie extensive deposits of coal and oil—bauxite, lead, zinc, iron and copper. New nuggets have recently been uncovered around the old gold mining town of Kalgoorlie. Nickel fields have been located in central Australia. Here the Pitjantjatjara tribes have been given 160,000 square kilometers (99,200 square miles) of land with guaranteed rights to all mining developments and royalties.

In the Northern Territory and West Australia rich uranium deposits have been located. Some of these deposits lie under land considered sacred by the Aboriginal tribes who live there. A similar arrangement with them has cleared the way for mining.

Meanwhile the great, silent platter of land dreams on, oblivious to the people scattered like marbles over its face, indifferent to the growing flurry of mining activities scarring its face. The sun beats upon it brazenly, the rose-colored willy-willies dance across its surface. Great gales scour it. Traceries of rain draw patterns over its seamed face. Droughts hammer it with mailed fists. And in its ever-present Dreamtime the heroes of which the old Aborigines sing continue to go about their deathless feats of replenishment and revitalization. It is the ancient Outback.

INDEX